Teach Yourself ASTROLOGY

LORD GANESHA AT TRINIDAD (WEST INDIES)

Published by
Lotus Press Publishers & Distributors

Teach Yourself ASTROLOGY

Pt. Gopal Sharma
Pracharya Sewa Ram Jaipuriap

4735/22, Prakash Deep Building,
Ansari Road, Daryaganj,
New Delhi - 110002

Lotus Press Publishers & Distributors
Unit No.220, 2nd Floor, 4735/22, Prakash Deep Building,
Ansari Road, Daryaganj, New Delhi - 110002
Ph.: 32903912, 23280047, 09811838000
E-mail : lotus_press@sify.com
Visit us : www.lotuspress.co.in

Teach Yourself Astrology

ISBN: 81-8382-040-9

Published by : **Lotus Press Publishers & Distributors**, New Delhi-110002
Printed at : **Bharat Offset Works**, Delhi

PREFACE

This book is an introduction to the basic symbols and language of Astrology, the very basic concepts that are the necessary foundation for understanding Astrology. Indian astrometaphysics is, as we have remarked elsewhere, superior to western notions of karma based merely on nodes. There is, for example, the accumulated karmas from all previous births, there is the karma allotted for this particular life, there is the remaining area of free will.

We all have a free will and we can create our own life. Astrology aims to increase our self-knowledge and enable us to work on our lives and increase our well-being. We must know what is wrong and where the foundations lie in order to improve things. Good as well as bad possibilities are mentioned in the description of the signs, houses and the aspects between the planets. It is up to each and every one of us to take advantage of the information Astrology gives us.

Enter a new dimension of spiritual self-discovery when you probe the mythic archetypes represented in your astrological birth chart. Myth has always been closely linked with astrology. Experience these myths and gain a deeper perspective on your eternal self.

Learn how the characteristics of the gods developed into the meanings associated with particular planets and signs. Look deeply into your own personal myths, and enjoy a living connection to the world of the deities within you. When you finally stand in the presence of an important archetype, the Creator will have something to tell you.

This is an excellent book that ties in syncretically, astrology, the planets, the Gods and Goddesses for whom the planets are named and many of the myths relating to them and indiviual signs. In short, it is one of the few concise, deep accounts of archetypal astrology ever written.

Dr. M.N Kedar
National Vice President
Rashtriya Jyotish Vigyan Parishad
Chennai (Regd.)

ACKNOWLEDGEMENTS

Besides all the ancient and modern scholars our deep gratitude and sincere thanks are due to Justice S. N. Kapoor and Dr. Prof. Shukdev Chaturvedi who have enlightened us with their knowledge and experience. Their moral support and cooperation was extremely valuable to us in preparation of this book.

Our friends, admirers, clients, readers and innumerable increasing letters also helped us in compiling this book for which we are grateful to all of them.

We are thankful to Acharya Chetan Sharma, Cheif Editor Jyotish Suman and Shri Vind Goel of Reliance Web World, who devoted a lot of time for material research and editing, leaving aside their own work.

We are extremely grateful to Sh. Gagan Aggarwal, President Aadi Shankaracharya Vedic Education Society & Rt. O. P. Bhardwaj, Vice-Chairman Institute of Vaastu & Joyful Living for their inspiration and encouragement to present this book in its beautiful get up for the enlightened readers.

Pracharya S. R. Jaipuria — *Pt. Gopal Sharma*

Best Selling Books by Pt. Gopal Sharma

1	*मोक्ष वाटिका*	50/-
2	*लक्ष्मी प्रवेश कैसे हो ?*	60/-
3	*सुगम वास्तु शास्त्र*	75/-
4	*प्रगतिशील वास्तु*	195/-
5	*श्री साई गृह वास्तु सूत्र*	120/-
6	*सफल जीवन में अंकों का महत्व*	75/-
7	*चमत्कारिक लक्ष्मी यंत्र (अंको का खजाना)*	125/-
8	*जानिये भविष्य आई–चिंग द्वारा एवं द्वार का प्रभाव*	60/-
9	*सुख का आधार वास्तु द्वारा सुधार बिना तोड़े–फोड*	30/-
10	*जानिए उपचार पायरा वास्तु तथा फेंग–शुई द्वारा*	90/-
11	*समृद्धि और सफलता के 108 सुनहरी उपाय*	75/-
12	*Advance Feng-shui*	195/-
13	*Progressive Vaastu*	225/-
14	*Wonders Of Numbers*	60/-
15	*Comprehensive Vaastu*	75/-
16	*Pyramid Power & Vaastu*	195/-
17	*Vaastu & Pyramidial Remedies*	195/-
18	*Sri Sai Science Of Gruha Vaastu*	195/-
19	*Vaastu Correction Without Demolition*	95/-
20	*Sri Sai Science Of Gruha Vaastu Model Plans*	350/-
21	*The Secrets Of A Happy Life Through Pyra-Vaastu & Feng-shui*	90/-
22	*The Magic Loshu Grid (Treasure Of Numbers)*	260/-
23	*Teach Yourself Vaastu*	150/-
24	*Teach Yourself Graphology*	150/-
25	*Teach Yourself Numerology*	125/-
26	*Awake Kundalini*	125/-
27	*Learn Meditation*	125/-
28	*108 Golden Tips For Love, Health, Wealth & Success*	75/-
29	*The Rationale Behind Indian Rituals & Beliefs*	168/-
30	*Advance Interior Designing Incorporating Vaastu & Feng-shui*	90/-

CONTENTS

1

INTRODUCTION TO ASTROLOGY

Astrology is the study of group of stars known as constellations — viz: nakshatra, which is a the method of increasing understanding through considering planetary forces, signs, etc., according to the knowledge within astrology. Astrology contains a great deal of knowledge regarding zodiac movements and its effects on people.

Medicine makes a claim that it is based on science, although it is unlikely it claims that it is itself a science. Although it claims to be based on science, it is estimated that no more than 1% of its procedures have been scientifically examined. In ones study, it was noticed that of the patients with clinically diagnosed cystitis eighty percent had an increased bacteria count in their bladders. However, twenty percent did not. In another study forty percent of men were found to have cancerous cells in their prostate glands, although forty percent of men do not develop cancer of the prostate. However astrology is a divine science percolated through God and rishis to propagate the planetary combination in conjuction to human affairs as well as past karma and its realisation in the present birth.

In scientific studies, twenty percent of women were shown to have reduced iron in their blood, although twenty percent of women aren't iron-deficient anaemic. These results are typical of results obtained in the human and social "sciences". It is very rare to get 100 per cent correlation between the factors being studied. Tendencies may be discovered, but absolutes are rarely found.

Such things as sciences, belief in witches, kinds of social behaviour, etc, do not just disappear because of some disproof. They go because there is a Paradigm shift. People no longer believe in witches and these sorts of beliefs just fade away. These major beliefs just fizzle out like an untended fire.

You cannot prove physics. You cannot prove the laws of physics. You cannot prove the theories of physics. All you can do is attempt to disprove the very specific hypotheses of physics which have been logically deduced from the theories (and perhaps from the laws). For example, at one time physicists believed that space contained a substance called the "ether". By measuring the speed of light in two directions, physicists demonstrated that the speed was the same, so there couldn't be a drag effect for the "ether". This meant the prediction from the "ether" theory had been disproved, on that occasion. However, beliefs about the ether still lurk in physics, and while there was a paradigm shift, like other paradigm shifts, it was not complete.

If science were simply empirical, then we would end up with a number of meaningless observations. The essence of science is the discovery or creation of laws and theories. These are ideas dreamed up by scientists and cannot be proved. One character of a scientific theory is that it can be disproved. If it cannot be disproved, then it isn't science. However, it cannot be proved.

These theories are not empirical. That is, you cannot observe theories and study them. They are beliefs that have explanatory power. However, the failure of an experiment to show the predictions are correct, does not disprove the theory. Nor does the success of the experiment in showing that the predictions are consistent with the experimental results prove the theory. They simply fail to disprove it.

A fundamental theory or assumption of science is the "theory of induction." This theory says that because all our observations show that the a theory is true then it is true, today, yesterday and tomorrow. We have every practical reason to "believe" that this is true. However, we have no logical proof.

The philosopher Bertrand Russell put it this way. A turkey who was also a scientist reasoned that because it had always been so in the past that he was fed every day, then he would be fed everyday in the future. Therefore, science is based on belief and not certainty.

Although science is modern man's religion, it is merely that. It is a religion or belief system that is not absolutely true. Roland Seidel, of Australian Skeptics, makes a number of interesting comments. "It is now a quaint relic that keeps the masses amused. It generates controversy, it captures imaginations, it may be a triviality or it may be dangerous but it is, after 120 years of formal research, unquestionably wrong."

Roland Siegel mentions that astrology could be dangerous in the sense that it could lead people to believe that what is written in the stars is inevitable, and cause them to give up when encountering events that might have been predicted in the stars. The same could be said of other practices, such as medicine, where a doctor giving an unfavourable prognosis might lead the patient to die.

Seidel suggests that there are three ways to test astrology:

1. Ask subjects to pick out their own horoscope from those of others,
2. Compare horoscope readings with personality tests,
3. Compare predicted events with actual events.

The first items presumes that natives can accurately pick out their own personality profile because they "know" themselves. It is an assumption that might not be true. Therefore, the inability of natives to pick out their own horoscopes may be a general phenomenon of subjects not knowing themselves.

The second test, likewise, is somewhat questionable. Personality tests created for specific purposes may not be applicable to astrological testing. A personality test devised to check for the astrological traits may be more reliable.

The third test, in principle, seems a valid one.

He mentions an experiment using 1000 subjects which compared birth data and the predictions of astrologers with measures of personality. There were no correlations, indicating that the birth chart does not predict the character of people. Astrology is claimed to be very general in what it says, so it is hard to tell whether it is true or not. A counter hypothesis here, is that subjects do not understand themselves very well. What might be overlooked here, is that the value of any personality testing might be drawn into question. It seems that any personality profile, providing it isn't too negative, will be accepted by the reader. This criticism of astrology is also a criticism of psychological testing in general.

Like all academic subjects, science is based on the element "air". It contains definitions and statements - qualities of air. Science is special in that it is pragmatic, that is concerns the earth element. In science, there are two elements that are despised. They are water and fire.

The scientist wants to appear logical (air) and practical (earth). Scientists do not want to appear to be "inspired" (fire) or "emotional" (water).

Most discoveries in science are, however, based on the despised elements. Many discoveries are "sudden intuitions" or result from dreams (water). Scientific reports are meant to be rational and pragmatic, so the way a scientist dreams up a theory (which uses water or fire) is often left out of the reports and the books. As the water of his mind began to clear, he saw, in ancient symbols (the Worm Oroubos) teach him how to understand the structure of benzene.

The astronomer, Kepler, was attracted to Copernicus's theory of the sun being the centre of the soloar system, not so much because of reason and facts (the decision is a paradigm shift, and not a scientific disproof) but because Kepler believed the sun was the "Father", space was the "Holy Ghost" and the planets were the "Sons of God". This belief inspired (fire) him to develop the theory.

The mathematician Poincare made one of his discovery in mathematics instantly as a fully blown cognition (fire). He says: "At the moment I put my foot on the steps the idea came to me, without anything in my former thought seeming to have paved the way for it, that the transformation I had used to define the Fuchsian functions were identical with those of non-Euclidian geometry."

Archimedes discovery of the principle of displacement is well known. He made the discovery instantly (fire), in the public baths and, according to legend, ran naked through the streets to his house, shouting "Eureka!" While science is concerned with intellectual understanding (air) and pragmatic proof (earth), the actual discoveries tend to occur in the areas of dreams (water) and instant intuition (fire). Of course without thinking about the subject, the scientists could not have had or understood their insights.

Astrology gives us a vocabulary and an understanding that enables us to better understand ourselves and other people, and, indeed, other subjects. We can learn that other people might view things differently from the way we see them. They may feel things or fail to see how our views are of any use at all. By understanding these people, we can increase our own development.

We should not be tied down by the horoscope. If a person acts and talks like a cancer, they are a cancerian type. Even if they aren't that type according to their chart. We can, and part of our development requires that we do learn to think, feel, act, etc in a variety of ways, or at least understand the other ways that others can think, feel, act, etc. Air signs and mercury are extremely important in our lives because they involve perception and communication, two essential skills or abilities in life. People like Van Gough and Helen Keller experienced extreme difficulty with a lack of these elements (or mercury well placed). This is the age of communication and people well endowed with communication skills can achieve more than those who lack these skills.

The point here is that modernisation becomes a place where words become more important than truth or ideas, as other people might see it. For example, laws are more words than justice. Mercury rules the words and Jupiter rules justice. The two are not the same. Similarly, for all the modern science in our lives, we still need a plumber to mend our heating system and a doctor to bandage our fingers. There is an illusory nature to our modern communication society.

Astrology can teach us that there are many kinds of people and that the one way suggested by a modern society is not the way that really suits everyone. It can suggest what "styles" of behaviour are common and which ones are being missed. The knowledge within astrology can be used without recourse to the practice of astrology, and world events and personal encounters, etc can be analysed and synthesised with this knowledge.

In the same way, the practice of astrology can be used with other knowledge bases. For example, the work of Bandler and Grinder in NLP can be used within astrology practice giving it an advantage of having a clearer therapy base. Of course this is only one example, and Jungian theories have been used as an astrology knowledge base in the past. Such are very interesting areas of development and expansion of astrology.

1.1. ORIGIN OF NUMBERS

Mathematics is a way of thinking and not a science. It is based upon assumptions or axioms (self evident truths) and proceeds using logic. The great unsolved mystery is how mathematics works because it originates in the mind rather than in empirical world. The deeper mystery is why logic works, even though it is similarly a thing of the mind rather than of pragmatics.

One mystery is the origin of numbers and how they come about. Animals seem to be limited in how they can use numbers. For example, it is said of birds, that they can count up to three, but not beyond. More than three is "many" or a "group". Therefore, a group of four hunters might approach a bird's nest. One hides and the others leave. The bird sees a "group" arrive and a "group" leave, so it returns to its nest to be shot by the fourth man.

Primitive people are similarly limited in their use of numbers and it is only with the growth of civilisation that our power with numbers increases. Von Neumann, the mathematical genius and protege proposed a theory of numbers in 1923. The consideration of emptiness results in the appearance of the empty set, which contains one member "emptiness". We therefore have the number one, and "emptiness". This makes two items. By having two items, we immediately create the idea of three items - "emptiness", one and two. In turn, this gives the idea of four—"emptiness", "one", "two", and "three". In this way all the numbers are generated from the conception of emptiness.

One property of numbers is that for every number, there is a greater number. The above paragraph shows that for every conception of a number, say "one", there is immediately the conception of a greater number, for example, "two". In this way, through the conception of "nothing", the whole raft of everything appears like a big bang, producing infinity.

Infinity is a number that is greater than any other number. For a bird, infinity is greater than 3, but for human mathematicians, who can in principle conceive of any number, the process of number generation always creates another greater number. So for human mathematicians, infinity cannot be stated as a number, but it probably can be so stated for birds, other animals, and primitive societies.

While there is nothingness, there is no thing. But the instant that nothingness is conceived or contemplated, then, as we saw before, there is the concept of one. And from here, all the numbers arise. The first number is zero, the egg-shaped number that represents nothing and everything. It is the sumbol for the universe.

The number two represents duality. It is a consequence of perception. In order to perceive there must be a perceiver and something to perceive. With two we have the dichotomies and the origin of conflict.

The number three is the number of harmony. It is the number for concepts and ideas. The being can see two things, which is a conflict, but when a third appears, then the being can see a harmony or middle point between the conflicts. The three is the number for concepts. In geometry, a figure with three sides is a triangle, and it is the first two-dimensional figure that encloses a space. In astrology, the harmonious aspect, the trine occurs when two planets are separated by 120°, which is the whole circle, divided by three.

The number four is the number of the universe. It is the first non-prime number. A prime number is a number that cannot be expressed as the product of other numbers, excluding one. All numbers can be expressed as the product of that number and one. Prime numbers cannot be expressed otherwise. Two can only be expressed as 2 × 1, and three can only be expressed as 3 × 1.

But four is the first non-prime number because it can be expressed as 2 × 2. The number four is therefore a higher harmonic of the number two, the number of dichotomy. The first three-dimensional figure (that is, one that encloses three-dimensional space) is the tetrahedron, which is made by joining four points (one of them must be outside the plane of the other three).

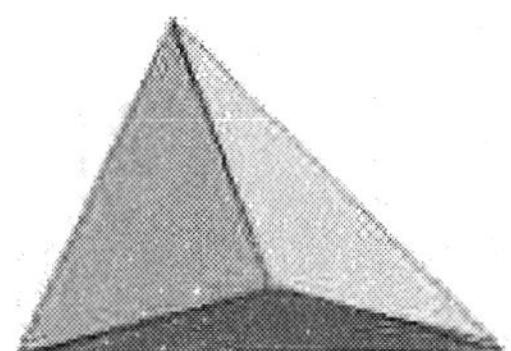

In the above figure is a tetrahedron (or four-sided figure). It is composed of triangles. There are four triangles which make the basic three-dimensional figure. In astrology, the square relationship between two planets occurs when they are separated by 90°, which is the whole circle divided by four, and it indicates a conflict.

1.2. VIEWING THE SKY

We can imagine how, in olden days, a man or a woman might stroll out into the night and ponder on the meaning of existence. They might gaze at the stars and wonder. They might notice something different or even spectacular in the skys and puzzle what it might mean. They might relate changes in the skies to happenings in their day-to-day world.

In almost all of these civilisations, there was advanced knowledge of the movement of the stars and the planets. The knowledge was advanced compared to the knowledge of the average person today. To the modern man in the street, the ability of the ancients to calculate the position and movements of the planets - even the precession of the equinoxes is a source of marvel. It is a source of marvel because modern city-living man may almost never see the moon and the stars - the city lighting and pollution hides them from his eyes. Many people in the modern world, therefore, are ignorant of direct experience of the heavenly phenomenon.

This man-made canopy of pollution and artificial light that obscurs the heavens deprives modern man of the direct experience of heavenly phenomenon and the opportunity to observe first-hand the role of the heavens in everyday life.

1.3. THE SEASONS

The following table shows the relationship between the seasons and the astrological signs:

Season North	Season South	Astronomical Time	Beginning	Middle	End
Spring	Autumn	March (Equinox)	Aries	Taurus	Gemini
Summer	Winter	June (Solstice)	Cancer	Leo	Virgo
Autumn	Spring	September (Equinox)	Libra	Scorpio	Sagittarius
Winter	Summer	December (Solstice)	Capricorn	Aquarius	Pisces

As the nights grow shorter and day and night become equal, the sun moves in the sign of Aries in late March and the astrological year begins with Spring. Aries is the beginning of Spring. It is a time of new growth and a time of greater light as the nights continue to grow shorter and the weather becomes warmer. By the time the sun has passed through Aries, in late April, plants are budding, animals are out of hibernation, birds have returned to northern areas and the soil is tilled and readied for planting. Aries is a time of rich new growth. A time of great energy and enthusiasm for the new year ahead. It becomes urgent to prepare the fields and set the seeds.

When the Sun reaches Taurus, in late April, Spring is established and new growth is everywhere. Birds build their nests and have their chicks, animals are born, and gardens are planted. This is a time of continuing toil as the fields are prepared and the seeds are set and cared for. The ending phase of Spring is signalled by the Sun moving into Gemini, in late May, when new life is dispersed locally and Summer is heralded. Many baby birds and animals have grown and are ready to fly away. The plants are established and work on the land becomes variable according to the needs of the farms.

Summer arrives when the sun moves into Cancer and the shortest day occurs. Life is lush and abundant, flowers and plants are in bloom. Food from the fields is ready to eat. It is a time to be protective over the land, because the work has been done and the crops are growing and others might come to steal the benefits of the work. Instinctive and basic urges are easily stimulated, both in response to threats and in caring for the young life.

In Leo the Summer is at its hottest. More food is available from the fields. And it is a time for parties and enjoyment. The people can live like kings and gain the advantages from the creative and impressive land.

In Virgo, the heat begins to be dissipated and the last of the crops are harvested. Although it is still Summer, the feeling that it will soon end is upon us. It is a time of work, preparing for the Winter and storing and preparing the food for the long nights to come. It is necessary to be analytical and critical of what has been done and what will be done to prepare for the future.

Autumn begins when the days are again of equal length and when the sun moves into Libra. It is a time to plan for winter. To weigh and balance the wherewithal to survive. It is the time to plan for the indoor life during the Winter. A partner to share the time during the dark time of the year. A time to be at one with Nature and all life forms, in the sense of accepting the reality that to survive, one must collect the harvest and store it for the times when there will be no food from the land. And a time to collect the seeds and plan to set them in the coming Spring. In many lands in ancient times, the people would not go to war until they had completed the harvest. This is a time, therefore, for diplomacy and harmony. It is a time for unity (or for war).

Over the next few months the plants begin to "die". The leaves are on the ground, and the trees are bare. In Scorpio ideas of life and death are most pronounced as the year's life is given up and new life is concentrated into seeds for the next year. The coming Winter threatens life and limb and Scorpio faces it without showing its fear. The emotions run deep and the need to discover the deep meaning and secrets is paramount. It is a deep and intense time because the time for preparing for the Winter is running out. It is also a secretive time, because others might try to find and steal your supplies of food, or the authorities might want to claim some of it. Hiding and discovering hidden things is therefore a time for Scorpio.

With the arrival of Sagittarius, the life energy is dispersed and the Autumn gradually changes to Winter. Some days are like Autumn, on other days the ground is covered by snow. This is the time of the hunter and the wanderer who travels far a field in search of meat to sustain life during the Winter. It is a time to be philosophical because little can be done now to prepare and survive the winter. Yet knowledge is valuable in finding additional food, such as that from hunting. Freedom and tolerance are practised because the time for passion and intensity have passed. Whereas the farmers might work in groups and follow strict rules, the hunter may go out alone and be under no-one's control.

The first signs of Winter come with the sun moving into Capricorn. This is signalled by the shortest day, when the nights are longest. It is the worst time in that the world is at its darkest, and it is also a new beginning, because after this, the nights will grow shorter as new light comes into the world. Capricorn is practical and plans for the future. Hard work during the dark days is Capricorn's strength. This is a time to be practical about the resources that are available. Capricorn is practical and prudently uses the resources available. In the early days of the year, it was a time optimism with the knowledge that Summer is coming and life and food is abundant. But at this time, there is no optimism, only the reality of what material things had been in store.

In Aquarius we experience the coldest days of the year. At this time, it may be necessary to stay indoors most of the time. It is a time of thinking and reflecting on the new year. With little to do outside, the Aquarian has time to invent new things and plan changes. It is also a time of waiting and controlling the emotions. The Spring is still far away, so at this time people dare not release their emotions. They become indifferent about most things as they await the Spring.

Pisces disperses the Winter and the nights become shorter and the days become longer. Some days are like Winter, whilst others are like Spring. It is a changeable time. Spring will soon come after the long Winter, so that people can become inspired with thoughts of the new year.

2

HISTORY OF ASTROLOGY

The use of a rising degree may or may not have been found in pre-Hellenistic Babylonian astrology. But the Hellenistic writers attributed the use of houses, or signs used as houses to Hermes. For Hermes we should understand a reference to Hellenistic Egyptian sources. It is probable that aspects are also Egyptian but we cannot say for certain. The lots are almost certainly Egyptian as well as most of the systems of rulership. Only the exaltations have a clearly Mesopotamian origin.

At any rate it is quite likely that the entire apparatus of horoscopic astrology was in place by 1 C.E., quite possibly several centuries earlier. Whatever may have been the language of Egyptian astrology when it first began to come into being, by 1 C.E. it was Greek. This is not to say that there were no astrology texts written in Coptic, the last form of ancient Egyptian, but no clear reference to any has survived.

All of the Egyptian texts that are referred to in the later literature seem to have been written in Greek. Possibly some were translations from Coptic. The use of Greek had important consequences. Although the Persian empire was a truly cosmopolitan empire with a considerable level of equality among the races that made up the empire, no one language came to predominate. No doubt Persian was used for official purposes, but Babylonian and Egyptian also continued to be used in their own areas in preference to Persian. But when Alexander the Great conquered all of Persia and Egypt, and advanced all the way into northwest India, Greek became the dominant language not only for official purposes, but also for any purpose that involved communicating from one ethnic area to another.

The original languages continued to be used for local purposes, such as Aramaic (which completely supplanted Babylonian) and Coptic. But a scholar or traveller could go anywhere from Greece in the West to India in the East and Egypt in the South and be understood. Any idea expressed in Greek could have a similar range of travel. Even after the Persian revival beginning first with the Parthians and later with the Sassanids, the Bactrian peoples of what is now Afghanistan and Pakistan continued to have Greek speaking rulers until the early centuries C.E.

Consequently the Babylonian methods embodied in Egyptian astrology as well as the Egyptian methods themselves could travel into India without difficulty. This accounts for the fact that all of the technical words in Indian astrology whose origins can be found in another language are Greek, not Babylonian, not Coptic, nor earlier Egyptian. What is also interesting is that there appear to be few, if any, technical words in Greek astrology that have their origins in any other language.

Below is a partial list of some of the terms in Hindu astrology that appear to have a Greek origin. All of the terms given below had Sanskrit equivalents which probably preceded the introduction of the words into India, and which also eventually completely displaced these words of Hellenic origin.

Zodiacal Signs

Sanskrit	Greek	English	Sanskrit	Greek	English
Kriya	Krios	Aries	Juka	Zugos	Libra
Tavura	Tauros	Taurus	Kaurpi	Skorpios	Scorpio
Jituma	Didumoi	Gemini	Taukshika	Toxotes	Sagittarius
Kulira	Karkinos	Cancer	Akokera	Aigokeres	Capricorn
Leya	Leon	Leo	Hridrogahoos	Hudroc	Aquarius
Pathona	Parthenos	Virgo	Chettha	Ichthues	Pisces

Planets

Sanskrit	Greek	English	Sanskrit	Greek	English
Hermnan	Hermes	Mercury	Ara	Ares	Mars
Asphujit	Aphrodite	Venus	Jeeva	Zeus	(Jove)
Heli	Helios	Sun	Kona	Kronos	Saturn

The following are terms for which there are no previous Sanskrit roots and appear to have come completely from Greek.

House and aspect words

Sanskrit	Greek	English	Sanskrit	Greek	English
Hora	Hora	Hour	Kendra	Kentron	Angle
Liptaka	Lepta	MInute	Panaphara	Epana phora	Succedent
Hiptaka	Hupogeion	Imum Coeli	Apoklima	Apoklima	Cadent
Jamitra	Diametros	Diameter	Drekana	Dekanos	Decan
Mesurana nema	Mesoura ven	Midhea	Sunapha	Sunaphe	Applying
Menyaiva	Meniaios	No equiv.	Anaphara	Anaphora	Separating
Trikona	Trigonon	Trine dhura	Dauraoria	Doruph	Doryphory
Dyuna	Dunon	Setting	Kema druma	Kenodro mia	Void of C.

This table indicates, these are all house and aspect words, indicating that this was an area of Hindu astrology on which Hellenistic astrology had great impact.

The question of the debt or lack thereof of Hindu astrology to Hellenistic is an extremely controversial one. This position is a bit hard to support given the above, and also given the very frequent references to the "Yavanas" who were Greeks or more precisely Greek speaking persons of various ethnic extractions.

David Pingree in his study of the Yavanajataka does an extremely thorough job of cataloging the parallels between the astrology of that work and that of the Greeks, and even he is forced to admit that there are many differences. However such differences do not require two different origins.

All it requires is a period of isolation between two branches of a tradition after an earlier period of unity, such that the two branches can diverge, and one, the eastern, merge with native traditions already in place. While we do not insist that Hindu astrology is entirely or even principally an offshoot of Hellenistic astrology, it must be said that the required period of isolation did occur which could have caused a single tradition to become two.

After 126 B.C.E. the Parthians, a Persian people, rose up against the Seleucids who succeeded Alexander the Great, and they reconquered most of the old Persian Empire except for the portion near the Mediterranean, and the portion in the northwest of India. The Parthians were extremely hostile to the Greeks (and later the Romans) and effectively cut off communication (or at least cut it down to a trickle) between the main body of Hellenistic people toward the West and the Bactrian Greeks in Afghanistan and Pakistan, who in turn remained in power until the early centuries C.E. The Bactrian Greeks eventually converted to Hinduism and their language disappeared. However as of about 200 C.E. they still existed as an identifiable group. These are the Yavanas of the Yavanajataka.

Still later the historian Kay mentions Hindu records from the 4th and 5th Centuries C.E. of a new Sun God cult coming in from the West. Given that Christianity displaced the worship of Sol Invictus, the Unconquered Sun, it is tempting to postulate that Hindu astrology received a second burst of input from a new group of Yavanas fleeing Christian persecution in the West.

The central problem is how much of Hindu astrology is indigenous and how much comes from the West. In any case it is very clear that whatever the Hindus got from the West they did not just take and passively apply. They altered, modified, and quite possibly improved whatever they may have received from the West and combined it with their own native traditions.

There is one other consequence of the Parthian separation. The Persian peoples had always been enthusiastic astrologers. It seems logical to conclude that they must have developed their own traditions from the astrology that they had inherited from the Mesopotamians and the Greeks. Then in 227 C.E. they were overthrown by the Sassanid Persians who would have continued the development of the Persian traditions of astrology.

Unfortunately when the Arabs came, almost all of the literature of the Zoroastrian Sassanids was destroyed. This includes their astrological works. However we do have a strong clue as to what their astrology must have been like. Most of the greatest astrologers in the Arab Era were Persians! And the astrology they taught is quite different from both the Hindu and the Greek. It had orbitss of aspect, the Great Cycles of Jupiter and Saturn, all of the elaborate systems of planetary interactions such as Refrenation, Frustration, Abscission of Light, Translation of Light and so forth.

While Arab era astrology clearly owes a large debt to Hellenistic astrology, it is also clear that in the two or three centuries between the last known Hellenistic astrologers and the first known Arab era ones, something new had come into the stream. This could have been, and probably was the Persian stream of astrology. And Arab Era astrology is the immediate ancestor of the Western astrology of today.

2.1. DEVELOPMENT OF ASTROLOGICAL STUDY

The oldest evidence of astrological study and practice are found within China. These developments predate those of Mesopotamia, dating back thousands of years. The ancient Chinese were meticulous in preserving their astrological records. Even today we may respect their comprehension of the heavens. By 2001 BCE the astronomers of China had determined the length of the year to be 365 days as well as the cardinal points of direction. They also clearly mapped the paths of the Sun and Moon well enough to predict eclipses.

Current records in Bharat indicate a well developed knowledge of astrology dating back to far ancient times. Remnants of work still exist from sometime around 3,500 BCE. Although most of the original manuscripts were lost, certain Astrologers reproduced their own versions of these earlier works. Some of these copies can be found in libraries belonging to Maharajahs.

Apparently, Indian astrology was held in very good standing elsewhere in the literate world of the time. In his book, Ancient Calendars and Constellations, E. M. Plunkett writes "The opinion of the Greek writers at the beginning of the Christian era may be quoted as showing the high estimation in which Indian astronomy was held. In The Life of Appollonius of Tyana, the Greek philosopher and astrologer, written by Philostratus about

210, the wisdom and learning of Appollonius are set high above his contemporaries because he had studied astronomy and astrology with the sages of India."

There is still much that remains unknown about the function of ancient megalithic monuments found throughout the world. In most cases it is still uncertain who the actual builders were. What we do know, from contemporary observations, is that most of these sites were used for astronomical observation. The dominant theory places their function within agricultural ritual.

Astrology's ancient beginnings are also traced to Mesopotamia at least as far back as 2001 BCE. These early records reveal a complex cosmology in which the Sun, the Moon and the planets represented Gods who possessed the power to direct and intervene in the course of physical events.

These early concepts progress through the growth of Babylonian civilization. Fundamental to this world view, was the idea that the planets had a divine nature and the ability to influence human destiny. The Babylonians established a pantheon of Gods, each possessing dominion over a particular area of human experience. For instance, Mercury, the god of the intellect was seen as quick and cunning, with a special quality of calculating intelligence. Mars was seen as the ruler of violence and war; Jupiter, a kingly figure and sovereign of men; Saturn, quick tempered and cruel. Here we can begin to recognize the basic forms of Astrology as we know it today. As Babylonian Astrology evolved, a correlation was recognized between happenings in the heavens and events on earth.

From ancient Babylonia, Astrology is fascinating, yet mysterious, Chaldeans. These Mesopotamian people are famed in history as magicians and sages. Two most noted figures were Belshazzar and Nebuchadnezzar. They reigned for nearly 100 years during the seventh century BCE. The Chaldeans were keen observers and mathematicians. They recognized that the events in the sky followed a pattern. They watched the stars move in fixed order across the heavens and the planets wandering in eccentric orbits, though in much the same plane. It was apparent to them that although the planets had their own individual movement they behaved in coherent cycles. It is here in Chaldea, that the charting patterns of the planets began. The very first Ephemeridae, tables of planetary motion, were constructed during the reign of King Assurbanipal.

In preparation of the new cosmological system, the Chaldeans made use of the twelve main constellations through which the Sun and Moon regularly pass. These were the precursors of the zodiac.

The great importance attached to the movements of the Sun, Moon, planets and stars was not limited to Asia and the Mediterranean basin. Throughout the world are found systems of Astrological study. In Western Europe this is attested to by the many megalithic sites spread across the continent, and in Britain. It has been documented that one of the principal functions of these sites was to compute the yearly movements of celestial bodies.

The monument at Stonehenge in England is perhaps, the most impressive of these sites. It possesses a sophisticated method of calculating a calendar with great accuracy. The positioning of its stones pinpoints the solstices and predicts eclipses. The layout of this stone circle was submitted to computer analysis, and a wide range of alignments were found showing this monument to be a gigantic megalithic computer. Radio carbon dates estimate that it was constructed about 2500 BCE. It is, indeed, a outstanding and baffling achievement for this Bronze age civilization.

Equally impressive, in its astronomical exactness, is the stone work of Newgrange in Ireland. Thought for a long time to be merely a large passage tomb, this 5,000 year old structure is in fact an observatory which the ancient Irish used to mark the solstice point of winter. Just before 9. A. M on each December 21, the shortest day of the year, the morning sun enters a small 8 inch portal and ignites the interior of this impressive mound. Evidence that these earlier people were not only skilled architects, but learned astronomers as well.

The Egyptian Pyramids remain singularly impressive to this day among all ancient astronomical buildings. They are aligned to the North Pole and the cardinal points. They were set so accurately, that a 1/12 degree deviation was discovered and accounted for by scientists as Africa's participation in the 'continental drift', rather than an error in Egyptian engineering.

The pyramids served a dual purpose; burial place of the pharaohs, and astrological calculators. There are sloping corridors leading from the faces into the interior. These were used as sighting tubes, allowing Egyptian astrologers to make naked-eye observations of great accuracy from which astrological calculations were progressed.

Important to the foundation of Greek Astrology, was a Babylonian, named Berosus, who lived about 250 BCE. His writings had a great influence on early astrological concepts in Greece. Unfortunately, no manuscripts of his work have survived. Bersosus established a school of Astrologers on the Island of Cos. During the next 400 years, the Greeks zealously converted Chaldean Astrology to their own traditions. Here, it became formal and complicated. The Greek tradition is credited with developing a system of diagnosis; and a method of calculating individual destinies based upon the moment of birth.

The Greeks also associated myths with the star groups. The heavens became an array of sacred objects, monsters, animals and heroes. They added human qualities to the heavens in constellation figures which embodied arrogance, love, fear, strength, compassion, vanity and tenderness. Alongside this mythologic view, another based on geometrical and mathematical relationships was seeded in Greece. Science began when the Greeks applied mathematics to the study of the heavens.

By about the third century BCE, Aristarchus calculated the distances to the Sun and Moon. His calculation for the Moon proved correct, but he was way off on the Sun. Still impressive, as he did this measuring without the availability of Instruments. Such tools were finally invented by Hipparchus. His instruments were so accurate that by 150 BCE he determined the length of the year to within six minutes. Three centuries later Ptolemy relied almost entirely on Hipparchus' data as the basis of his world system. Ptolemy constructed a model of the universe that could explain the retrograde movements of the planets as well as the variations in their speed and brightness. The Ptolemaic model of the universe dominated Western thought for over 1400 years. The first textbook of Astrology, The Tetrabiblos, was written by Ptolemy.

In 1543, it was Copernicus who put the sun at the center of the universe. This was the same premise that had been held by Aristarchus in the middle of the third century. Old ways die hard, and the Copernicus system was not accepted for another 100 years. It was the work of both Kepler and Newton that dealt the death blow to the Ptolemaic system. Kepler found that the planets actually move in ellipses, not circles, and Newton explained why. Kepler believed only those people who had never studied astrology could possibly deny it.

In 1687, Issaac Newton's book 'Principia Mathematica' opened the door to the modern era of studying the heavens, called astronomy. This was the beginning of the decline astrology would suffer until the mid-19th century.

3

VEDIC ASTROLOGY

Vedic astrology is an ancient behavioral analysis and forecasting system. It employs a diagram of the positions of the planets relative to the earth and sky, based on the time and place of a person's birth. The astrologer, depending on skill and clarity of consciousness, makes inferences regarding an individual's disposition and character and may foretell events in that person's life. Using advanced techniques, an astrologer may even forecast events on a community, national, or global scale.

What draws people to astrology through the ages, is the desire to make the right decisions. Plagued with poor decision-making capabilities, a person can retreat and inordinately reduce their expectations. Taking lower risks, they attain lower results, lower rewards, and basically, a life of diminished joy.

Astrologers help their clients understand whether they are in a slump or a surge and what might be the anticipated duration of either one. Astrologers, as counselors, want to help lead their clients to positive outcomes and to help them build a psychology that naturally triggers life-supporting behaviors.

Ultimately, the best way to get out of trouble is not to get into trouble to start with. Patanjali, the author of the

"Yoga Sutras", offered a timely aphorism: "Avoid the danger which has not come yet:" Vedic astrology offers us a map to guide our life and gives us an analytical time profile of our behaviour to help us understand what compells us to act. Vedic astrology helps us determine which behavioural traits to promote and which ones to target for self improvement.

At the time and place of birth, there is a specific astronomical pattern in the heavens. This sky model is recorded from a distinct geographical point. Astrologers document this planet-earth-sky pattern and call it a chart. On the chart, they mark significant features such as the following:

1. Where the planets are in the sky — by listing their location in a constellation, or sign of the zodiac.
2. The location on the earth — by using latitude and longitude; these are called houses.
3. Which sign is on the horizon, or that part of the sky east of the birth location, at the time of birth — this point is called the rising sign or ascendant.

The above are the three most significant components of a chart. As the earth rotates, the signs move through the houses, following the clock throughout the day. The birth diagram is called a horoscope (from Greek horo, indicating time, and scope, meaning to look at). In India, the chart is called the chakra (wheel), Janma Kundali (rising), or Kala Purusha (body of time). In Vedic astrology, a chart is drawn as a square and/or a box of triangles, but in Western astrology, it is drawn as a wheel.

The birth chart diagram is interpreted according to specific rules of Vedic astrology as laid out by the ancient rishis, or seers, such as Maharishi Parasara. Fundamentally, Vedic astrology, or Jyotish, is a system for interpreting how behaviour will unfold over time.

Modern Western psychology analyzes behaviour, but Vedic astrology shows how behaviour might change over time. Life patterns seen in the birth chart are matched by the astrologer against the patterns seen in historical rules and records of parallel astronomical information.

For predictive purposes, the Jyotishi uses a Vedic planetary almanac, or a computer program, to track the location of planets from sign to sign, and house to house, to locate when circumstances will emerge. An astrologer determines when a planet will cross a sensitive point in the birth chart, stimulating a specific event.

This event, waiting in the storehouse of that person's destiny, occurs as promised in the birth chart, modified somewhat by actions performed in this life. While these events are not necessarily predestined or even required to happen, they show a tendency to do so over the course of a person's life. The chart is a record of that person's karma.

The astrologer's role is to match the patterns in the birth chart with the current patterns in the heavens, and to understand the nature of that person's environment. The astrologer consults the records in the ancient texts, much of which is memorized, and then analyzes, synthesizes, and draws a conclusion about the events at hand. The correctness of the reading is directly proportional to the experience and spiritual advancement of the astrologer, as well as to the recipient's desire and receptivity to having their chart read clearly. The reading is a short-term partnership.

Planets actually cause events to happen. They attempt to scientifically verify astrology with references to gravity, cosmic radiation, and the like. The Vedic texts declare that Vishnu, the great maintainer of the universe, incarnated and reincarnated in cycles born of the essence of the nine planets. Brahma, the creator, acting on behalf of Vishnu, uses the planets in specific ways to disperse the creation around the universe.

The Vedic system is a more accurate astronomical representation of the Sun's position in relation to the skies. The Western systems emphasize the relationship of the Sun to the earth and the seasons. For this reason, Western astrology can be referred to as "tropical astrology", and Vedic astrology can be called "sidereal astrology." Sidereal astrology simply means that planetary movements are tracked against the positions of the stars, thus favouring the astral positions.

Over the last several hundred years, this difference has caused the two systems to drift apart by about 24 degrees on where they mark the start of an astrological year. Both use the vernal or spring equinox as the start, but in Vedic systems, the vernal equinox currently marks 6 degrees of the Sun in Pisces — this is 24 degrees back from where western astrologers mark the equinox as the beginning of Aries.

The difference between the Western start of the astrological year in Aries, and the Vedic or sidereal start in Pisces, is called the ayanamsa. Ayanamsa means "division of the year". Unless you were born between about the 15th and 20th of the month, you will find your "Western" Sun has most likely moved back by one sign in a Vedic astrological chart. Vedic scholars have differences of opinion as to the exact date and time when the two systems started drifting away from each other.

Vedic astrology traditionally uses one house system, called the "equal house" system. (There is another system, called the Bhava Chalita, which adjusts the size of the houses according to the latitude of the birth place.) In Western astrology, there are numerous methods for dividing up the earth's latitude and longitude and forming the astrological land and time divisions called the houses.

Vedic, sidereal astrology also incorporates star signs based on the movement of the moon — about one day per Sun sign. These 27 moon signs are called nakshatras. Vedic astrology also divides the ecliptic, or the Sun's path, into 15 additional divisions, so we not only have the 30 degree divisions of each Sun sign, but further divisions of up to 150 segments. These are called the Shodasavargas. It's like having an additional 15 birth charts to read from.

Vedic astrology also distinguishes itself in its predictive tools. Of especial note is the 120-year cycle forecasting system called the Vimshottari Dasa, where each planet is allotted a specific period of influence in the chart and is used to forecast more deeply into the nature of an individual's future.

Vedic astrology is also integrated into Hindu societal functions and remains to this day an accepted part of religion and of most daily life. It is not uncommon to see heads of state as key speakers at Vedic astrology conferences. Many modern Indian business managers and computer experts working in the United States still wear astrological pendants to bring them success.

Vedic astrology is also a companion system to Ayurveda, the major health care system of India. In fact, Vaidyas, or "doctors" of Ayurveda, often consult the astrological chart of a client to seek additional diagnostic information. Vastu, the art of architectural measurement and placement (similar to China's Feng Shui), can be linked to the astrological tendencies of an individual's birth chart.

Vedic astrology has its roots in consciousness, and so remedial measures can be taken, which can include religious performances (yagyas, pujas, and shantis); gemstones; mantras; charitable acts; gandarvaveda musical renditions; stotras (prayers); vratas (vows); herbs; and mineral concoctions (bashmas). All of these corrective measures are held to counterbalance the negative impressions from previous actions (samskaras).

4

ASTRONOMICAL ASTROLOGY

4.1. TIME

Time is often thought to be a difficult concept to define simply or to say what it is. Time can be defined operationally. The day is related to the time the Sun takes to apparently revolve around the earth, and the year is related to the seasons. Civil clocks must reflect the day and civil calendars must reflect the seasons.

4.1.1. Leap Years

Our calendar making began in 46 BC with Julius Caesar, and this system is called the Julian system. Every 4th year, a day was added to the calendar, to make a leap year. This system was accurate to 0.0078 days each year. Over a century, this amounts to an error of about 3/4 of a day. By the 16th Century, the error was such that the beginning of Spring shifted from March 23rd to March 11th. To correct this, Pope Gregory XIII introduced the Gregorian system in 1582, which made Spring start on 21st of March and used a more sophisticated system of leap years. The Gregorian calendar year is, on average, 365.2425 days in length. It will take about 3,300 years before this calendar is out of step by one day. The

Gregorian system is the system we use in our civil calendars.

In the civil calendar, the year must be a whole number of days (by convention). The real year is approximately 365¼ days. Every 4th year we add on a day to make up for the difference between the tropical year (real year) and the civil year. Every new century, if it is divisible by 400, an extra day is added.

4.1.2. Sidereal Time

While a civil day is 24 hours, a real day is slightly longer. It is approximately 4 minutes longer. A real day is measured by the stars and is called Sidereal Time. A sidereal year is therefore approximately 366¼ days.

4.2. THE MOON

While we have only mentioned one way of telling the time at night using the stars, there are many ways of doing this. You can, however, tell the time at night in areas where the Sun isn't visible by observing the Moon. The table below shows drawings of the Moon from the new Moon to the waxing crescent.

4.2.1. Moon Phases

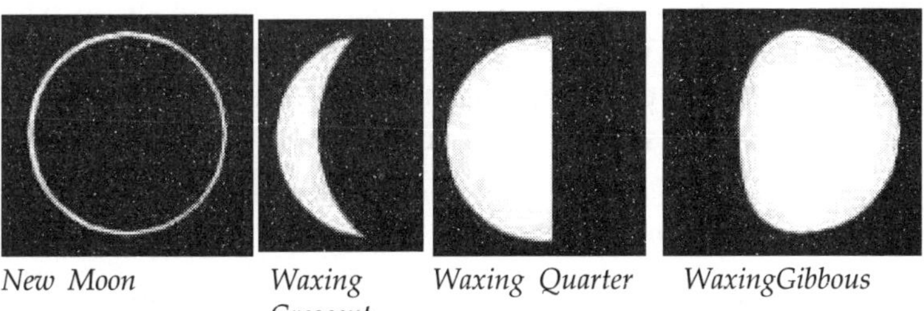

New Moon *Waxing Crescent* *Waxing Quarter* *WaxingGibbous*

When the Moon is gradually showing more and more of its illuminated surface, we say that it is waxing, which also means "to grow in size, strength and power". When the Moon is gradually showing less and less of its illuminated surface, we say it is waning, which also means "to decrease in size, strength and power." The Moon is gibbous when it is more than half illuminated and less than full. The word gibbous means "humpbacked". This waxing and waning phase of Moon is called Shukla Paksh and Krishna Paksh respectively in Hindu astrology.

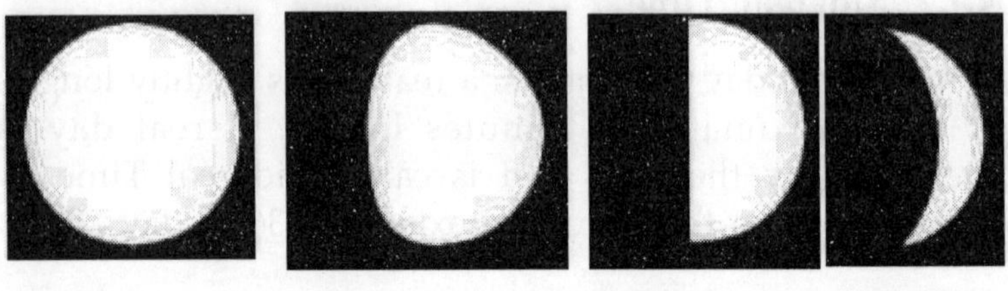

Full Moon *Waxing Gibbous* *Waxing Quarter* *Waxing crescent*

The Moon repeats its cycle approximately every 29½ days. This figure is slightly less than the average number of days in a month, so occasionally there are two full Moons in a month. This occurs approximately every 2.7 years. When this second occurrence of the Moon in a month occurs, it is called a blue Moon. It therefore follows that "once in a blue Moon" means once every 2.7 years.)

Each season normally has 3 full Moons. Occassionally, there are four. For religious purposes, it is the third Moon in a four Moon season that is considered the odd one out.

4.2.1.1. Time from the Moon

You can tell the time from the Moon, because the phases of the Moon are the result of the relative position of the Sun and the Moon. This means that the position of the Sun below the horizon can be determined by the phase of the Moon. When the Moon is new, the Sun is behind the Moon, and the Moon sets and rises approximately at the same time as the Sun. When the Moon is full, the Sun is opposite the Moon, and the Moon rises when the Sun sets (approximately). In these case, the Sun is 180 degrees opposite the position of the Moon. In other cases, where the Moon is a crescent, quarter or gibbous, the Sun's position can be determined from the Moon's position. And by knowing the Sun's position, we can determine the time. The Moon, therefore acts as an indicator of the Sun's position. The following figure shows this in greater detail. Half of the Moon is always illuminated by the Sun (barring eclipses, etc). So the Moon phases appear to us as crescents, gibbous, etc, because of the angle between the Moon and the Sun.

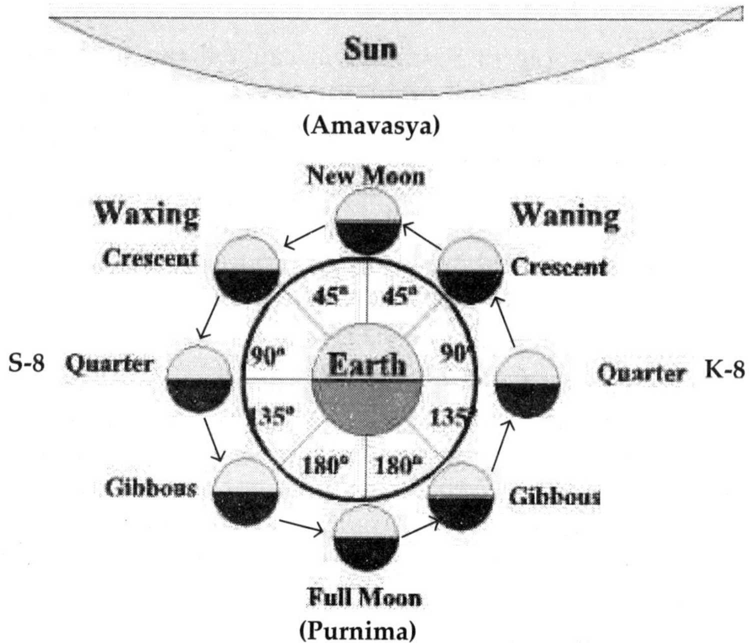

The figure above, which isn't to size or scale, of course, considers the Sun to be stationary and the Moon to move.

When the Moon is in line with the Sun and between it and the earth, then there is a new Moon. When the Sun and the Moon are in line with the earth in between, then there is a full noon. Between this are the other phases. When is the Moon is at 90° to the Sun, then it will be a half-Moon. The crescent and the gibbous are at 45° and 135° respectively.

Because the Moon isn't always visible at night (unlike the stars, which almost always are visible, weather permitting), the Moon is less useful as a means of telling time. For example, when there is a new Moon, theMoon and the Sun set at almost the same time, so the Moon no more available than the Sun.

4.2.1.2. Time from the stars

While the people in Scandinavia can tell the time from the Sun all day and all night, in other parts of the world, we cannot see the Sun at night. However, there are various ways of telling the time from the stars. One way to do this is to use the Pole Star and the Big Dipper or the Plow. It is sometimes said that the Pole Star is the brightest star in the sky, however, this isn't true. It is sometimes easier to find the Big Dipper and then to find the Pole Star from the Big Dipper.

You can find the Pole Star by drawing an imaginary line through the two stars that make up the end of the "bowl" in the Big Dipper (or the end of the plow) and follow it for about 5 times the apparent distance between these two stars. You will be led to the Pole Star. The names of the two stars are Arabic names: Dubhe and Merak.

The point is that this line will rotate like the hands of a big 24 hour clock and from the angle of this clock hand, you can determine the time. If you imagine the first time reading as a reading on a normal clock and then, say an hour or two later estimate the time on this clock, you can estimate the difference in time between these two readings. Because this is a 24 hour clock, you will have to double the estimated time to get the real difference in hours. It is better to imagine a normal clock, because imagining a 24 hour clock is difficult when we are used to the normal 12 hour clock.

You can easily create some things to help you tell time from the Big Dipper Clock. You could, however, tell the time without any tools at all. The first thing you need to know is that the clock will show 12 'O' clock on March 7th, so for every month thereafter you add one hour to the apparent time. You do this because the Big Dipper Clock keeps Star (or Sidereal) time. The star days are 4 minutes longer than our days, so sidereal time is about 2 hours per month faster than our regular time.

You can estimate the time from scratch by estimating normal time and adding one hour for each month after March. You then double the result to get the time from the stars. To get normal clock time, you will need to know what time the Sun is at its highest. This will vary with localities and may involve Summer Time corrections in civil time. So in some areas the Sun is at its highest at 1 pm in Summer, in others, the time may be different.

When you estimate time in this way, you will be able to tell the time within, say an hour. If you use simple equipment with which to read the Star Time, you can be much more accurate. The Ancient Egyptions measured time very accurately and they could determine Sunrise within a few seconds.

There is a big clock (or even several) in the sky with which you can determine Star Time. Civil or clock time is always related to this Star Clock. While some elements of time are arbitrary (for example, the 24 hour day and the 60 minute hour), the length of the day is real in terms of the movements of the stars and the movements of the Sun. While our normal clocks and civil time relate to Solar Time, the big clock in the sky works on Sidereal Time.

4.2.1.3. Time without a clock.

Modern city dwellers may never see the stars and the Moon, and have become detached from the sky. They probably think that time is what a clock says. Yet we used the idea of time long before there were clocks, and some primitive people today tell the time by pointing to the Sun. Even though they do not have or understand clocks, they may answer the question, "When will you return?" by pointing to the position the Sun will be in when they return.

The method of pointing to the Sun doesn't always work. It works best near the equator where the Sun keeps its apparent position for different times throughout the year, irrespective of the seasons. The Egyptians and Babylonians divided the hours of the night and the hours of the day each into 12 hours. So at certain times of the year, an hour was long as 75 minutes during the night and as low as 45 minutes during the day, and vice versa, depending on the seasons.

Although the path of the Sun varies in different areas of the earth, the highest point is always the same in the sense that it indicates noon. Where the Sun is not directly overhead, the noon mark would be the place of the Sun when it was noon. So when it was over a certain mountain, say, the time would be midday or noon. Other markers were used for other times of the day. In different seasons, the Sun would be above the markers, although it would be higher over the marker in Summer than it would be in Winter.

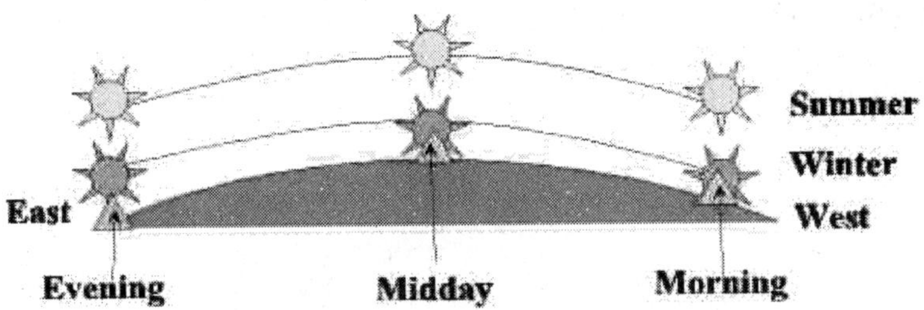

In the above diagram, the perspective is from the Northern hemisphere. Morning and evening markers would be reversed in the Southern hemisphere, as would East and West. The reason for this is that we look South for the Sun, in the Northern hemisphere, and we look North for the Sun in the Southern hemisphere. The grey triangles refer to markers, which could be mountains, etc. On or near the equator, the Sun would be "straight up", so telling the time from the Sun is easier and markers aren't needed.

The markers work from a given location - house, farm, etc - and new markers would be needed elsewhere. These markers were often used in Scandinavian countries. They would have the advantage of seeing some light from the Sun, even at night, and so another marker could be made for midnight. Using markers in this way, people could tell the time throughout the day and the night through all the seasons.

In a similar way, people would tell the time by the position of the Sun in relation to their houses. For example, in a given house, the Sun may shine into a room from a certain direction at a given time. So when the Sun is shining into the room in a given direction the owner will know it is, say, 4 pm.

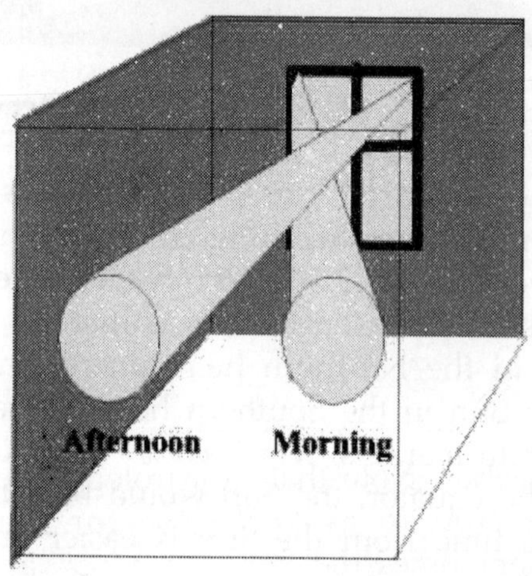

In a South facing room in the Northern hemisphere, the Sun might indicate the time through a South-facing window by illuminating different parts of the room at different times of the day. Time is in some ways reals and is independant of clocks. It is something we can, if we are aware, notice from our environment. The Sun moves in an apparently clockwise manner across the sky in a consistent manner such that we can tell the time even without clocks or knowledge of clocks. High in the Northern hemisphere, people can tell the time from the Sun whether it is day or night (because the Sun is never greatly distant from the horizon and its rays can be seen, even in the middle of the night).

The ancient Egyptions could tell the time very precisely, so they could know and be prepared in their rituals for the exact moment that the Sun (the Sun God, Ra) would rise. However, in Egypt has no midnight Sun, so they had to use the stars.

5

SOLAR SYSTEM IN ASTROLOGY

In traditional Western astrology, the planets have the significances listed below. These significances have been handed down since ancient times and come from Ptolemy's *Tetrabiblos*. Note that in astrology, the Sun and Moon are referred to as "planets" for the sake of convenience. Sometimes the Sun and Moon are referred to as *The Lights* or the *luminaries*.

5.1. THE SUN

According to Marcus Manilius (1st century AD) in his epic (8000 verses) poem *Astronomica,* the Sun is benign and favourable, and presides over the head. It is usually thought to represent the conscious ego, the self, and the principles of creativity, spontaneity, health and vitality - the life force. The Sun is the planetary ruler of Leo. In Chinese astrology, it represents Yang. In Indian astrology, Sun is called as Surya, the God of Sunday.

5.2. THE MOON

According to Manilius, the Moon is melancholic, and presides over the right arm. The Moon is the ruling planet of Cancer. In astrology, the Moon is thought to be associated with a person's emotional make-up, unconscious habits, rhythms, memories, and moods. It is also associated with emotions in general, the mother, maternal instincts or the urge to nurture, the home, and the past. In Chinese astrology, it represents Yin. In Indian astrology , Moon is called as Soma, the God of Monday.

5.3. MERCURY

In Western astrology, Mercury is the ruling planet of Gemini and Virgo. According to Manilius, it is an inconstant, vivacious, and curious planet that presides over the right leg. Called "the winged messenger" in Alan Leo's book *What is a Horoscope?*, Mercury represents the principles of mentality, thinking patterns, rationality, transport, reasoning, and communication. This follows from the planet being named after the Roman messenger god. In Chinese astrology, Mercury is ruled by the element water. In Indian astrology it is called 'Budh' related to 'Budhi'i.e intelligence.

5.4. VENUS

Since the Roman goddess Venus is the goddess of love, in Western astrology the planet Venus is also associated with love. Venus is also associated with the principles of harmony, beauty, balance and the urge to unite. According to Marcus Manilius, Venus is generous and fecund, and presides over the left arm. In Gustav Holst's musical composition *The Planets*, Venus is called "The Bringer of Peace". Venus is the ruling planet of Taurus and Libra. In Chinese astrology, Venus is associated with the element metal. In Indian astrology, Venus is a female planet, known as Shukra, the God of Friday.

5.5. MARS

According to Manilius, the planet Mars is ardent, and

presides over the genitals. Called "The Bringer Of War" in Alan Leo's *What is a Horoscope?*, since the planet is associated with the Roman god of war, Mars in Western astrology is associated with confident and aggressive personalities. It is also associated with the principles of energy, ambition and drive.

Mars is considered the ruling planet of Aries. Before the discovery of the planet Pluto, it was also considered the ruler of Scorpio. Most modern astrologers consider Pluto the ruler of Scorpio, but may regard Mars as a co-ruler, while some more traditional astrologers still regard Mars as the only ruler of Scorpio. In Chinese astrology, Mars is ruled by the element fire. In Indian astrology, Mars is called Mangal, the God of Tuesday.

5.6. JUPITER

In Western astrology, the planet Jupiter is associated with merrymaking. According to Manilius, Jupiter is temperate and benign, and presides over the stomach. Called "The Bringer Of Jollity" in Alan Leo's book *What is a Horoscope?*, Jupiter is the ruling planet of Sagittarius, and was also that of Pisces prior to the discovery of Neptune. Many astrologers still consider Jupiter to be the Planetary Ruler of both Sagittarius and Pisces. In Indian astrology, Jupiter is known as Guru or Brihaspati, and is the Lord of Thursday. In Chinese astrology, Jupiter is ruled by the element wood. Jupiter is associated with the principles of growth, expansion, faith, prosperity and protecting roles.

5.7. SATURN

In Western astrology, Saturn is the Ruling Planet of Capricorn. According to Manilius, Saturn is sad, morose and cold, and presides over the left leg. It is associated with the principles of limitation, restrictions, boundaries, reality, crystallizing and structures. Before the discovery of Uranus, Saturn was also the ruling planet of Aquarius; however, many astrologers still use Saturn as the planetary ruler of both Capricorn and Aquarius. Saturn is called "the Bringer Of Old Age" in Alan Leo's book *What is a Horoscope?*, and is considered to represent the part of a person concerned with long-term planning. The Saturn return (*The Return of Saturn*) is said to mark significant events in each person's life.

In Chinese astrology, Saturn is ruled by the element Earth. In Indian astrology, Saturn is called Shani, and the bringer of bad luck and the God of Saturday.

5.8. URANUS

For some modern Western astrologers, the planet Uranus is the ruling planet of Aquarius. Manilius was unaware of the planet's existence, because it was discovered only in 1781 by Sir William Herschel. Uranus is associated with the principles of genius, new and unconventional ideas, discoveries, inventions, radical politics. Around the period of discovery in 1781, the idea of democracy and the human rights was prevalent, with the breakaway of the US from England and a few years later in 1789, the French revolution.

5.9. NEPTUNE

The planet Neptune is associated with illusion, deception, religions, spirituality, the mass media, music, drugs, extreme sensitivity, psychic phenomena and altered mental states. The discovery of Neptune in 1846 coincided with the discovery of anesthetics and hypnotism around this period.

For some Western astrologers, Neptune is the ruling planet of Pisces. Prior to the discovery of Neptune, Jupiter was considered the ruler of Pisces, and some modern astrologers consider Jupiter a co-ruler of Pisces. Some astrologers do not believe that Neptune rules any particular sign, even though they may use the planet in chart interpretation.

5.10. PLUTO

To some modern Western astrologers, Pluto is the ruling planet of Scorpio. Called "the great renewer", Pluto is considered to represent the part of a person that destroys in order to renew. A commonly used keyword for Pluto is "transformation." Many (traditional and modern) astrologers do not use Pluto as a ruling planet but do use the planet for chart interpretation and predictive work. Pluto is also associated with extreme power and corruption and the discovery of Pluto in 1930 coincided with the rise of Fascism in Europe and the major proliferation of organized crime in the USA. It is also associated with nuclear armament which had its genesis in the research of that decade.

5.11. ASTEROIDS AND MODERN PLANETS

While some astrologers trace the roots of astrology to ancient Babylonia, the ancients only knew of the five naked-eye planets, plus the Sun and Moon. Modern telescopes have revealed many bodies that are incorporated into the predictions of astrologers, and some that are not. Uranus, Neptune, and Pluto are relatively modern planets, with Pluto having been discovered in the twentieth century. Three new planet-sized bodies, Sedna, Quaoar, and 2003-UB313/Xena, have been discovered in the 21st century but not yet incorporated into mainstream astrological predictions. Some asteroids, such as Vesta and Ceres, might qualify as planets by some definitions, but are nearly universally ignored by astrologers.

6

CALCULATIONS

The calculations performed in astrology involve some skill in arithmetic and simple geometry and serve to locate the apparent location of heavenly bodies on desired dates and times based on tables constructed by astronomers. There have been astrologers who claim to try to put astrology on a sound scientific basis, but for most it is an art that merges calculations with their own intuitive perceptions. For most astrologers the purported relationship between the celestial bodies and events on earth need not be causal, nor even scientific.

6.1. ROUGH CALCULATIONS

As in all walks of life, it is easy, even for highly skilled people, to do something really silly. There are certain obvious things about a chart, which can be used to check that the chart is reasonably accurate. Some of these rough calculations are very rough, but they do produce a rough idea and they can identify major errors.

It should be routine to check the obvious about all charts. It is also true, that even if you are talking to someone who knows only their birth date, you can reasonably guess certain things about their chart.

6.1.1. Sun Signs

When looking at a chart, check the Sun sign accords with the birth date. The actual dates vary slightly by a day or two. But the last week of a month and the first three weeks of the next month tend to be in the same sign. Below is a list of approximate dates for each of the twelve signs:

Sun Sign	Approximate dates
Aries	21 March - 19 April
Taurus	20 April - 20 May
Gemini	21 May - 20 June
Cancer	21 June - 22 July
Leo	23 July -22 Aug
Virgo	23 Aug. - 22 Sept
Libra	23 Sept. - 22 Oct
Scorpio	23 Oct. - 21 Nov
Sagittarius	22 Nov. - Dec. 21
Capricorn	22 Dec. - 19 Jan
Aquarius	20 Jan. - 18 Feb
Pisces	19 Feb. - 20 March

For instance, Aries is often March 21st to April 19th. So a person born between these dates will have their Sun in Aries. If they were born on April 19th, clearly their Sun would be about 29 degrees of Aries. If on March 21st, then we would expect about 0 degrees of Aries. Actually a person born at 10pm on 20/mar/1990, for example, would be Aries. So this is approximate. But if a person born on 19th of April said they were Aries, it is believable, although perhaps they are Taurus? But they certainly aren't Pisces or Leo!

So the first guess or check is to ask whether the sign and the birth date are reasonable. Do be careful of historical dates, as the date in the Julian Calendar is 11 or more days behind the date in the Gregorian Calendar. For example, Leonardo da Vinci was born on 15 April 1452, which is a Julian date. This means, he is a Taurian, and not Aries!

6.1.2. Degree

Roughly, the degree of the Sun is the number of days the Sun has been in the sign. For instance, if someone said they were born on 31st July, we would know they are Leo, and expect their degree to be 8 because:

1. Leo is Leo 23 July -22 Aug, and
2. 31st July is 8 days on from the 23 July

Actually 31st July 1997 had the Sun at 7degrees 50 minutes at the start, and 8 degrees 48 at the end of the day, but normally we would expect to be accurate within a degree or two.

6.1.3. House System

The division of the houses will clearly depend on the House System used. For instance it will be different for Placidus (normal system) from the equal house system. The Houses changes about every two hours. This is accurate for the Equal House System only, and is a guess for Placidus and other systems.

The Sun in the chart represents its position in the sky, although East in the chart is on the left, and West is on the right, opposite the normal! If the person is born about dawn, their Sun will be near the first house cusp, and for a birth within 2 hours before dawn, the Sun will be in the first house. So if dawn is 6am, then if they are born between 4 am and 6 am, their Sun will be in the first house (approximately, if the Placidean Houses are used). If they are born after dawn, within 2 hours, they will have their Sun in the twelfth house.

If they are born at midday, they will have their Sun near the tenth house cusp (MC). And if they are born at Sunset, their Sun will be in the seventh house cusp.

If they are born at night, their Sun will be in the lower part of the chart, and if in the day, in the upper part.

If they are born in the evening, then their Sun will be in the Fifth House. If in the early morning, in the Second House.

6.1.4. Ascendant

If the Sun is in Libra, that is she was born between Sept 23 and Oct 22, then at Sunrise, the Ascendant will be about 0 degrees of Libra. So if she was born about 6 am, if this is dawn, then her Ascendant will be in Libra, or possibly Virgo.

6.1.5. Mercury and Venus

Mercury is always in the same sign as the Sun or in the neighbouring signs. So if the Sun is in Gemini, then Mercury will be in Taurus, Gemini or Cancer. This is because Mercury is never more than 28 degrees from the Sun. So if someone says they were a Gemini, and there Mercury is in Aries, you would be suspicious (it can't be), and if they said their Mercury was in Scorpio, you would know they were wrong.

Similarly, because Venus is never more than 48 degrees from the Sun, it will always be with 2 signs of the Sun. So if the Sun is in Virgo, then Venus is in Virgo, Cancer, Leo, Libra or Scorpio. This doesn't tell us much, but it does tell is that a Virgo with Venus in Capricorn has something wrong with the chart!

6.1.6. Retrograde Planets

The outer planets (Mars, Jupiter, Saturn, etc) are

retrograde when they are opposite the Sun in the chart. That is, in the opposite half of the chart. That is, within a sign or two of the opposite sign to the Sun sign.

The inner planets are retrograde when they are between the Sun and the earth, but this isn't detectable on the chart.

The "points", such as the Moon's node, do not follow these rules. We can conclude here that there is something wrong with a chart which shows the outer planets retrograde, when they are in the same half of the chart as the Sun. Similarly, if they are opposite the Sun (or within a sign of this), then we expect them to be retrograde.

6.2. CALCULATING THE ASCENDANT

The ascendant is the sign on the Eastern horizon when the birth occurred. For example, Mary was born 7 May 1982 at 11 hours 17 minutes AM, New Berlin, New York, USA. The longitude is 75 degrees, 20 minutes west of Greenwich. And the latitude is 42 degrees 37 minutes North of the equator. We have already calculated Mary's sidereal time of birth, so all we have to do is to look in the tables of houses to find the ascendant. Mary's sidereal time of birth is:

1 hour 16 minutes 13 seconds

The tables depend of the latitude of birth, so we need to look at the tables for the nearest latitude to Mary's place of birth. The American Ephemeris 1931 to 1980 contains tables of houses which we can use. There are, of course, many other sources. The tables are organised in terms of time, each time 4 minutes different from the previous, and in terms of latitude, each latitude 1 degree different from the previous.

You can look at the tables and pick the nearest ascendant. As the time is nearer 1 hours 16, you can choose to look at the table for 1 hours 16. As the latitude is nearer to 43 than to 42, you can choose to take the value from the tables for latitude 43. The result from the tables is 5le19. The correct answer (5le9) can be computed.

6.2.1. Accurate Computation of the Ascendant

To explain the principle here, the table below, which has simple numbers to illustrate the procedure. Remember these are not real ascendants, etc. Let us also imagine that the native was born at 1 hour 18 minutes sidereal time, and at a latitude of 42.5 degrees. These are some imaginary figures:

Latitude	1 hour 16 mins	1 hour 20 mins
42 degrees	4	8
43 degrees	6	10

First the native was born at 42.5 degrees, which is half way between the two values we have above. That is half way between 4 and 6. So the mean ascendant at 42.5 latitude and at 1 hour 16 minutes is 5. Similarly, the mean latitude at 1 hour 20 minutes is the mean value of 8 and 10, which is 9. So we have the two mean ascendants at the two times These ascendants are 5 and 9. These are the ascendants at 42.5 for the two times above. To find the actual ascendant we need to find the average of these two values, which is 7.

Let's look at the real example of Mary. Mary was born 37 arcminutes after the first latitude of 42 degrees. The two latitudes above differ by 60 arcminutes. So the factor for Mary is 37/60 or 0.6167. The difference between the two ascendants (4le47 and 5le19) is 32 arcminutes.

We multiply this by the factor by the difference:

32 × 0.6167= 19.73, say 20

We add this to the lower latitude's ascendant (4le47) so:

4 le 47+20= 5 le 7

We do the same for the second time. In this case we have 5le34 and 6le5. The difference is:

31 arcminutes

Multiplying this by the same factor as before (0.6167) we get

31 × 0.6167=19.12 or 19

So we get the ascendant at the higher time as:

5le34+19 = 5le53

Mary was born (sidereal time) 1 hour 16 minutes 13 seconds. The difference in the two times is 4 minutes or 240 seconds. The proportion is 13/240, or 0.05417. The difference between the two mean ascendants (5le7 and 5le53) is 46 arcminutes. The amount to add to the lower value is:

46 × 0.05417=2.49 or about 2.

So we add this to the lower value:

5le7+2= 5 le 9

6.2.2. Southern Hemisphere

The ascendant is the sign on the Eastern horizon when the birth occurred. For example, Kiri Te Kanawa born in Gisborne, New Zealand on Monday 6 March 1944 at 2pm. TZ:12.00, Lat 38S40, Long 178E01. We have already calculated Kiri's sidereal time of birth, so all we have to do is to look in the tables of houses to find the ascendant. Kiri's sidereal time of birth is: 12 hours 46 minutes 48 seconds.

This has already been corrected for a Southern birth. We procede to calculate the Ascendant in the same way we did for a Northern Hemisphere birth ... except, we reverse the signs. So if the sign is Aries, we take Libra. If the sign is Scorpio, we take Taurus. And similarly, we take the opposite sign. The tables depend of the latitude of birth, so we need to look at the tables for the nearest latitude to Kiri's place of birth.

The American Ephemeris 1931 to 1980 contains tables of houses which we can use. There are, of course, many other sources. The tables are organised in terms of time, each time 4 minutes different from the previous, and in terms of latitude, each latitude 1 degree different from the previous.

You can look at the tables and pick the nearest ascendant. As the time is nearer 12 hours 48, you can choose to look at the table for 12 hours 48. As the latitude is nearer to 39 than to 38, you can choose to take the value from the tables for latitude 39. The result from the tables is 22sa21. We need to reverse the sign here for a Southern birth. So the answer would then be 22ge21. The correct answer (22ge18) can be computed.

6.2.3. Accurate Computation

Kiri was born 40 arcminutes after the first latitude of 38

degress. The two latitudes above differ by 38 arcminutes. So the factor for Kiri is 40/60 or 0.6667. The difference between the two ascendants (22ge7 and 21ge29) is -38 arcminutes. We multiply this by the factor by the difference:

$$-38 \times 0.6667 = -25.33, \text{ say } -25$$

We subtract this from the lower latitude's ascendant (22ge7) so:

22ge7-25= 21ge42

We do the same for the second time. In this case we have 23ge0 and 22ge21. The difference is:

-39 arcminutes

Multiplying this by the same factor as before (0.6667) we get

$$-39 \times 0.6667 = 26.00 \text{ or } 26 \text{ arcminutes}$$

So we get the ascendant at the higher time as:

23ge0-26= 22ge34

Kiri was born (sidereal time) 12 hours 46 minutes 48 seconds. The difference in the two times is 4 minutes or 240 seconds. Kiri was born 2 minutes 48 seconds after the first time in the tables, or 168 seconds. The time factor is, therefore, 168/240, or 0.7000. The difference between the two mean ascendants (21ge42 and 22ge34) is 52 arcminutes. The amount to add to the lower value is:

$$52 \times 0.7000 = 36.40 \text{ or about } 36.$$

So we add this to the lower value:

21ge42+36=22ge18

22ge18 is the correct ascendant.

6.3. CALCULATING THE CHART—UT OR GMT

While few people are actually going to work out astrological charts by hand, that is, using paper, pencil, it is important to know how to do it. It may also be true, that unless an astrologer spends a great deal of time doing charts by hand, they will never fully understand astrology. By doing charts by hand, you will begin to understand more about the movement of the planets and how they combine to affect the lives of people on Earth.

Another reason is that astrology is a sacred science and by doing the mundane routine things, our minds enter a meditative state wherein we realise things we might not have been able to know or understand otherwise. The tools you require to make a horoscope are (in addition to writing and drawing tools) are an atlas and an ephemeris. An ephemeris is a book or booklet containing information about the positions of the planets, etc.

The information you require is the date and time and place of birth. The place of birth is expressed in longitude and latitude. Universal Time, or *Greenwich Mean Time,* is required to calculate the positions of the planets.

6.3.1. Universal Time

Suppose someone is born in New Berlin on 7 May, 1982, at 11:17 according to the hospital clock. This is the Civil Time of birth (Clock time). At Greenwich, the time will be different. It will be later than this civil time because the

Sun has already passed over Greenwich and the civil time is some hours later than the civil time at Greenwich.

Universal Time is the time at Greenwich for the given civil time, taking into account any daylight saving time.

6.3.1.1. Calculating universal time

For example, Miny was born 7 May 1982 at 11 hours 17 minutes AM, New Berlin, New York, USA. Perhaps you think everyone knows that New York is in the USA, but do be careful. Many place names are duplicated, especially between the USA and European countries. So don't be afraid of the obvious.

Now use an atlas to look up the longitude and latitude for this place. we get:

75W20

And for the latitude:

42N37

That is, it is the longitude is 75 degrees, 20 minutes west of Greenwich. And the latitude is 42 degrees 37 minutes North of the equator.

Eastern Standard Time (EST) for New York is based on 75 degrees longitude. That is 5 hours (75/15=5). When it is 7 am in New York, it is 12 noon in Greenwich, because New York is west of Greenwich. For western longitudes, add the time difference to the local time. (And for eastern longitudes, subtract the time difference). We need to find the time at Greenwich (GMT) in order to calculate the chart. Because the Sun rises in the east, the times in the east are earlier than those in Greenwich, and those to the west are later than Greenwich.

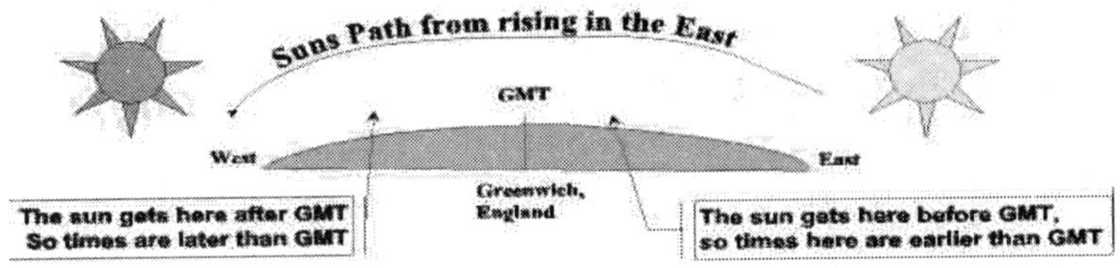

Sun movement diagram

If you look at the figure above, you will notice that the Sun is in the East. It hasn't reached Greenwich yet, so the time in the East is earlier than that at Greenwich. The Sun will reach Greenwich before it reaches places in the West, so places in the West have a time later than those in Greenwich. So if you live to the East of Greenwich, then the Sun rises earlier, and you get your noon before Greenwich does. If you live to the West, then you get your noon later than Greenwich. Therefore, Greenwich Mean Time (GMT) is later for those in the West and earlier for those in the East. This GMT of birth is also called Universal Time.

Longitude	75W	GMT	75E
Time Difference	+5	0	-5
Local Time	7 AM	Noon	5 PM

So if you were born at 7 AM at longitude 75 West, it would be noon at Greenwich (7am +5 hours). Similarly, if you were born at 5 PM at longitude 75 East, it would be noon in Greenwich (5pm - 5 hours).

6.3.1.2. Summer time

In some countries, time is changed to take advantage of the light and this is called Daylight Saving Time. When this is in force, you often need to subtract one hour (although sometimes 1/2 hour or 2 hours). In summer time the clocks are advanced one hour, so we need to remove this hour, when summer time is in existence. Summer time was in existence for our example, so the GMT time of birth was:

16 hours 17 minutes - 1 hour = 15 hours 17 minutes GMT

For example, Jhoney was born in Gisborne, New Zealand on 6 March 1944 at 2pm. The longitude is 178E01 and the time zone is 12. Daylight saving was not in operation. The birth occurred in the East, so we subtract the time zone. The UT was:

14 hours - 12 hours = 2 hours (2 am)

That is, universal time was 2 am (time on the Greenwich meridian).

6.3.1.3. Near midnight birth

Charles Aznavour was born in Paris on May 22, 1924 at 0:15 am. The longitude is: 002E20, and the time zone is 1. The birth was in the East, so the time zone is subtracted from the birth time (civil time):

0 hours 15 minutes (quarter past midnight) - 1 hours

Add 24 hours so we can subtract 1 hour:

24 hours 15 minutes (quarter past midnight) - 1 hours = 23 hours 15 minutes

That is, 11:15 pm on 21 May 1924 - the Universal Time here is the day before the civil day of birth.

6.3.1.4. Next-day birth

A birth occurred in New York, NY, United States of America on Tuesday 26 June 1990 at 20:03.The latitude is 40N43 and the longitude is 74W00. The time zone is 5 and daylight saving was in operation. Because the birth in West, the time zone is subtracted. Taking into account summer saving the UT of birth is:

20 hours 3 minutes +5 (Time Zone) - 1 (Daylight Saving) = 24 hours 3 minutes

Because the time is greater than 24, we subtract 24 and add one to the day. So the UT birth time is:

0:03 am on 27 June, 1990.

6.3.1.5. Local mean time

LMT is required to calculate the house positions (the ascendant, in particular). It is the accurate local time. For example a baby was born 7 May 1982 at 11 hours 17 minutes AM, New Berlin, New York, USA. She was born very close to the time zone of 75 degrees, but she was born 20 arc minutes to the west of this zonem (75W20), so her Sun rose a little later than shown for the time zone.

The Sun moves 15 degrees for every hour. So it moves one degree in four minutes of time. It therefore moves 4÷3 minutes of time for every 20 seconds of arc. Her local mean time of birth is therefore:

11 hours 17 minutes (Civil Time of birth) -

1 minute 20 seconds (longitude correction, calculated above) -

1 hour (Summer time) = 10 hours 15 minutes 40 seconds (local mean time)

So she was born at 10 hours 15 minutes and 40 seconds. When we convert to GMT, we add the allowance for longitude West and subtract for longitude East. In contrast, when we convert to local time, we subtract the allowance for births West of the Time Zone, and add for births that are East of the Time Zone.

6.4. CALCULATING THE POSITION OF THE PLANETS

Whereas the precise calculation of the house cusps requires a lot of detailed work, which is not really warranted from the accuracy of the birth data, the position of the planets can be easily calculated from tables. For example, a baby was born 7 May 1982 at 11 hours 17 minutes AM, New Berlin, New York, USA. The longitude is 75 degrees, 20 minutes west of Greenwich. And the latitude is 42 degrees 37 minutes North of the equator. Her LST is 1 hour 16 minutes 13 seconds. GMT birth time: 15:18:20

While we needed the local sidereal time to calculate the position of the house cusps, we need the GMT time of birth to calculate the positions of the planets. In this example, the following information from an ephemeris. She was born at 15 hours 17 minutes UT then the actual position of her Sun will be calculated using this as a fraction of 24 hours. This fraction is approximately 15.2833/24 or 0.6368. We therefore get, with the midnight ephemeris:

Sun	Position in Taurus
Sun 7 may 1982	16:06:57
Sun 8 may 1982	17:04:59
Fraction	0.6375
Difference in arc	00:58:02
Proportion (0.6368 × 00:58:02)	00:37:00
Sun pos	16:43:57

The Sun is, therefore, in 16 ta 44, rounding up to minutes. In a similar manner we can calculate the positions of the rest of the planets:

Planet	Birth Position	Sign	07 May 1982	08 May 1982	Factor
☉ Sun	16:43:57	ta	16:06:57	17:04:59	0.6368
☽ Moon	12:16:49	vi	04:26:48	16:44:05	
☊ North node	14:56:41	ca	15:03:08	14:53:01	
☿ Mercury	07:51:28	ge	07:10:01	08:15:02	
♀ Venus	03:28:47	ar	02:46:03	03:53:05	
♂ Mars	00:27:52	li R	00:31:05	00:26:02	
♃ Jupiter	03:59:34	sc R	04:04:04	03:57:01	
♄ Saturn	16:51:33	li, R	16:54:04	16:50:07	
♅ Uranus	03:17:11	sa, R	03:19:01	03:16:08	
♆ Neptune	26:39	sa, R	26:40:00	26:38:08	
♇ Pluto	24:57	li	24:58:03	25:56:08	

Those with an **R** in the sign are retrograde planets.

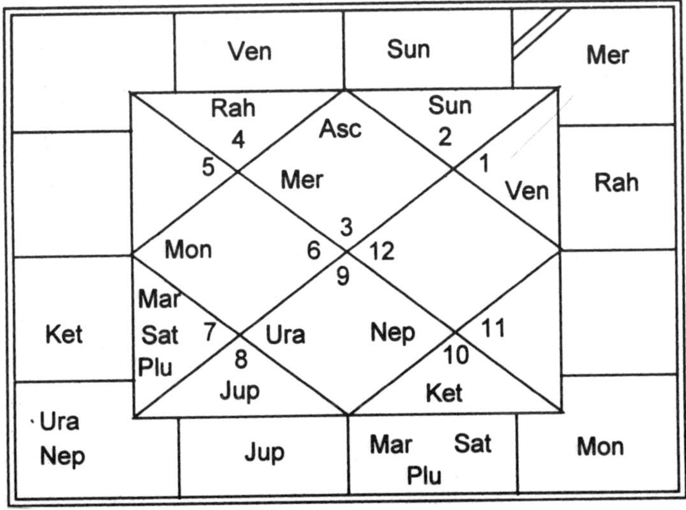

7

SUN SIGNS

Western astrology employs the tropical zodiac which divides the ecliptic into twelve signs of equal length starting at the first point of Aries, which is defined as the point at which the ecliptic (the apparent path of the Sun through the heavens) crosses the celestial equator at the spring equinox. It is important to note that these signs are completely independent of the astronomical constellations after which they were originally named and no longer bear any relationship to them.

When the Sun is in one of these signs, then the basic nature of the person is shown in the way of the sign. When the Moon is in one of these signs, then the instinctive reactions of the person are expressed in the way of the sign. And similarly for the planets and the houses. By understanding the signs, we can increase our ability to understand others, and we can also learn other ways of thinking and behaving. All people born into a country or an area which is rules by a given sign tend to have some of the characteristics of that sign. Also the way we are is influenced by the signs of those we are most in contact with.

7.1. ARIES

Aries rules the head, the cerebral hemispheres, the upper

jaw, the eyes, and the face. If you were born when the Sun was in the sign Aries, the Ram, then you are likely to be an initiator of action, a doer. You may be someone who is assertive and says what you think, or you may be someone who goes on and invents something, even if it isn't something world shattering. You are not someone who figures things out in minute detail in advance. You have an idea come to you and you have to act on it. You are direct in what you say or do and you do things with passion or enthusiasm. Sometimes you have an overwhelming urge to do something (even if you aren't sure why you want to do it!)

♈

You have a childlike tendency to see things from your own point of view and to express yourself as you see things in an innocent and youthful way. While some might see this as being self-absorbed or even selfish, you see it as being honest and expressing your true thoughts and feeling and doing what you think is right.

You are likely to have an abundance of energy to do what you have in mind or what is burning inside you and demanding action.

You are independant in the sense that you consider what motivates you rather than to do what others might want you to do. In what you do you are earnest and determined.

You may have a clear idea of what is right and what is wrong. You tend not to see the various shades of grey that others seems to be involved in. For you it is clear and you must get on and do it.

You may find you are a good motivator of others. As an Arian, you don't say what you think will please, you say what you think is right and true. In this way, you can get others to follow you. Others may interpret this as being dominant and aggressive, while you see it as expressing yourself.

Some Arians can be in tune with life and seem to do things at the right time even though it appears that they are acting spontaneously and without detailed consideration and thought. You will probably have done it before you get round to thinking about it!

You have the capability to be an executive and as such you will chase your goals with enthusiasm and passion, sticking to your goal. You probably have the tendency to be discouraged, or to get bored, though. And you may leave behind you a trail of things that have been left undone. You need to be aware of this tendency and really work on maintaining and completing what you set out to do, even after the passion subsides, which it does for Arians.

Arians can be quick to anger, and equally quick to forgive. Also as a leader you need to learn to consider how other people think about things and try to see things from their point of view. You need to work on the Libran skills - the charm and balance that comes naturally to them.

Arians are idealistic in the sense that they have a clear idea of what is right and wrong and what should be done. Arians are great initiators and pioneers and anything new is fascinating to them. One image of the Arian is that they will explore new worlds and new lands, both physically, mentally and spiritually. They will go where "Angels fear to tread".

In a negative way, Arians can be seen as being aggressive, cocky, dominating and intimidating. Sometimes this is true (negative Aries) but often it is the way that Aries is seen by the other signs. What is over-confident and reckless to one person can be self-assertive and bold to another.

Because Aries are guileless, they may blurt out things that they would not have said had they thought about it. And they can be upset later when they think these things over. They can be too quick to jump to conclusions, have poor judgment and stubornly refuse to face the truth. They can live in a fantasy world where the realities of life do not affect them. You see Arians see their own point of view, but have to work on seeing the point of view of others. While sticking to your guns and following your ideals is a way to achieve things, it is also a way of failing because you do not accept the feedback from others. Once again, Arians need to learn the skills of the other signs, particularly those of Libra.

7.2. TAURUS

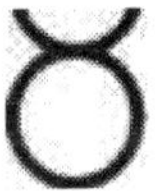

Taurus rules the neck, the ears, palate, larynx, tonsils, thyroid gland, lower jaw, occipital region, cerebellum, atlas, and cervical vertebrae, vocal chords, carotid arteries, jugular vein, and the pharynx. If you were born when the Sun was in Taurus, then you are likely to be strong-willed, persevering and steadfast. The symbol for Taurus is the bull, and when you are determined you are like a bull, and in a charge, nothing can stop you. You may appear fairly calm and relaxed, but when something gets you going, then other people had better watch out. You are practical and grounded and show a great deal of discipline. You can be cooperative, artistic and even idealistic.

The persistence of Taurus, compared with Aries, is strong and fixed. Whereas the Arians are quick to take action and follow their passion, the Taurians are slow to get started, but once they have built up their momentum, they are much more persistent in chasing their goals. The difference between Aries and Taurus here, is that Arians are quick to get started, whereas Taurians are slow. Taurians are concerned with practical and realistic ideas as they relate to their personal resources and wealth. Arians act in relation to motivations and enthusiasm, whereas Taurians are much more thoughtful in a practical way. They are cautious and careful in what they do.

As a Taurian, you are idealistic in a practical way. You may dream of building something which is real and can be visualised - something tangible; whereas Arians, for example, are idealistic about an idea that fills them with passion and motivation. The idealism of Aries is fiery, whereas the idealism of Taurus is down-to-earth.

Taurians are well known for their concern with personal resources and wealth and Taurus's greatest fear is loss and poverty. For this reason they tend to be thrifty, and others might see this as being stingy or miserly. They see it as prudence and carefulness.

Taurians are steady,composed, courteous and even charming. They can appear as slow to other signs. They are dependable and loyal and seek to conserve what they have. They are scrupulous and honest in what they do, although this is a practical kind of honesty.

Taurians are productive. They can be charming, affectionate and sometimes generous. They are calm and thoughtful in a practical way. Taurians, because they don't like change, can be seen as bigotted, unbudgeable, and somnetines addictive. Taurians can be fascistic - Adolf Hitler was a Taurian!

7.3. GEMINI

Gemini rules the arms, hands, shoulders, lungs, thymus gland, upper ribs, trachea, bronchi, capillaries, breath, and oxygenation of the blood. People born when the Sun is in Gemini are adaptable and versatile. They can cope with many things by changing or

II

presenting a different face. They are intellectual and competent with language as it relates to the everyday world. They are intellectual in the sense that they tend to be abstract and general in their thinking. Geminis are restless and may even be nervous. They are always active and doing things and should avoid exhausting themselves.

Geminis are flexible and able to deal with change. They deal with change in the sense that they can move onto other things and have the capability to act and react in various ways. They tend to be fluent in language and are good talkers and speakers. London Mayor, Ken Livingstone is a Gemini.

Geminis are bright, ingenious and perceptive. They can be imaginative and inventive, especially in language and communication generally. They are rarely stuck for words and can improvise expertly. They are young, even when old, at least in their hearts. They have a charming innocence and thirst for understanding, especially in everyday matters rather than deep and profound matters.

Geminis are poets and reasoners. They are good at logic and rationality. They are especially humorous. They are persuaders and educators, especially school teachers. Geminis can be viewed as impatient and stimulus craving. They may be thought as dabblers rather than serious students or workers. They can be deceptive and manipulative. While they may be considered as lawless, they often make good lawyers.

7.4. CANCER

Cancer rules the stomach, diaphragm, the breasts. It also rules the upper lobes of the liver, thoracic duct, peristalsis, the pancreas, gastric vein, and the serum of the blood. Cancer, like Aries, is one of the cardinal (initiating) signs. Cancers are

♋

instinctive and protective and homely people. However, in relation to whatever they class as the home, the can be very active in obtaining, establishing and maintaining the home.

The symbol for Cancer is the crab. The crab carries it home around with it and defends anyone (or any other crab) that tries to take the home away from it. Another symbol for Cancer is the turtle. A key phrase for cancer is "I feel" and Cancer's can be moody or crabby. Those born under the sign of Cancer, tend to be caring, nurturing and sensitive people. They are especially sensitive in relationship to the home. They are loving, caring and protective. A Cancer person may show these qualities in relation to the family and the home, or might consider his or her country or business their home and behave in these ways in relationship to their country or home.

Cancers are very supportive and good at listening and empathising with others. They are good with emotions, both their own and those of others. Cancer people are maternal and loyal and they are tenacious in manners that they feel strongly about. Cancers are psychic and responsive. They are attached to their mothers (or nurturing parent) but also like to travel, so long as they know that their home is safe.

Other signs may be to some degree psychic, but Cancer is psychic in the sense of having feelings or intuitions. Whereas the intuitions of Aries are fiery and enthusiastic, those of Cancer are more emotional and to do with feeling that something is right or true. To some signs it sounds strange to say, "I feel this is true", because they believe that truth isn't a feeling, but a mental understanding. However, to Cancer, it IS a feeling. In fact, almost all things in the lives of Cancer peoples are feelings (or emotions) rather than intellectual, practical or enthusiasms. Cancers can be loyal and patriotic (when they probably Feel their country is their home). The are also passionate and romantic, often in a sentimental way. These people can be gentle, humorous and kind.

Cancers are self-reliant and often have good memories. To others, Cancers may appear to be passive-aggressive, panicky, hypersensitive, hysterical or projecting. Some people actually have these qualities, but often these qualities are how the cancer person appears to other signs. Signs that lack the qualities of cancer need to learn to be more emotional, less dry, more youthful, and learn to develop rapport with children, both their own psychological inner child, and with real children in the outer world.

7.5. LEO

Leo rules the heart, aorta, vena cava, dorsal region of the spine and spinal cord. The symbol for Leo is the lion. And Leo is a regal sign. It does not mean that all kings and queens are born under the sign of Leo, but it means that those who are so born have a regal manner. That is they like to be the centre of attention as if they were holding court. This is the sign of the actor (whether professional or in everyday life - Leo's may try to make everything they do or say impressive and creative. Winston Churchill (Moon in Leo), Napoleon and Mussolini are all Leos.

Leo's, like Taurus, are extremely persevering and strong-willed. While Taurians are steadfast in matters relating to personal resources, Leo's are steadfast in matters relating to performance and procedure. While one modern image of Leo is the stage- or screen-actor, this does not mean that Leo's are stage, etc, actors or even interested in public performance. Lucille Ball, Gracie Allen, Mae West, Dustin Hoffman, Mick Jagger Madonna and Alfred Hitchcock are all Leos. It means that they behave like the archetypal actor who appears on stage bigger than life to capture the audience. Real Leos can perform in this way in any occupational group. So a top scientist might act in a Leo manner, commanding attention and taking things over.

Leo's unlike Aries, are more stable or fixed in their way of behaving and in chasing their goals. Leos are really persistent. They can maintain their position whereas Arians might go off and do something else. Leos are intuitive in the way that Arians are, that is, they can get an idea in their head and be driven by enthusiasm to do or to maintain that idea. For Leos these ideas are held and supported extremely strongly. Like Arians, Leos are passionate and direct in their communications and behaviour.

Leos are self-centred in that they judge truth and right from their own standards, but they are more other-centred than Aries. They will listen to the other person's point of view, even if they still go on and do their own thing. They are full of life and energy and expressive. Leos can be seen as dominating and authoritarian while they see themselves as confident and honest. They are loyal, generous and kind and can even be supportive.

They are certainly entertaining, humorous and dramatic, although others can see them as vain, exhibitionistic show-offs. Thos who lack Leo qualities can be seen as being detached and repressed and over-submissive. They are unconscious of their appearance and the effect they have on others. Leos have the gift of enlightening others with their radiance, and need to learn to allow others to radiate too.

7.6. VIRGO

Virgo rules the abdominal region, intestines, the lower lobes of the liver, the spleen, the duodenum, and the sympathetic nervous system.

The symbol for Virgo is the virgin. It is often a symbol for someone who seeks to serve (or help) others and who does not have great ego demands on life. Virgos ♍ are detailed, analytical and critical. This means that they tend to analyse things so they can understand their parts. They are critical in the sense that critical means to evaluate. They are also synthesising in that they take the analysis or the parts and generalise it to a rule. Virgos can take a single incident and turn it into a law of nature!

Like Geminis, Sagittarians and Pisceans, Virgos are adaptable, so they can cope with awkward situations or lives, generally by getting on with their work or service. Virgos can be restless and always on the go. Virgos, like Taureans and Capricorns, are very practical. Unlike Taureans, Virgos are not particularly concerned with personal resources, although they will help Taureans gain personal resources. They are more concerned with practical work and procedures. Unlike Capricorns, Virgos do not seek personal ambitions, and are not egotists.

The keyphrase for Virgo is "I analyse". If a Virgo is given a generality, he or she will analyse it into its parts and offer criticisms. If an Arian gives a pronouncement full of enthusiasm and passion, the Virgo will want to know where the idea came from and how it relates to the facts. Virgos will examine these in a down-to-earth manner and will think about it in a practical rather than an enthusiastic manner.

Quite clearly, Virgos are disciplined and will follow procedures precisely. They are also perfectionists and will find it hard to know when they are finished or when they have achieved their goal. They are like the painter who never thinks his or her picture has been completed and continues to fiddle with it.

While the sign Virgo can sound like the sign of a slave or someone who works for others, and Virgos are other-centred, this isn't true. Sean Connery and Aristotle Onassis are Virgos. The idea of "service" with Virgo means an attention to detail, discipline and step by step actions. These and the other Virgo qualites can be used at any level of society. Mother Theresa and Queen Elizabeth are Virgos.

When we think of Virgo we think of someone who is extremely well organised, meticulous and precise in what they do. Others might see this as being a critical perfectionist, and it may annoy some other signs. Virgos are logical and practically rational, and they are hard-working and dependable. While they see themselves as discerning, others might see them as dissatisfied and fussy. Other signs might view them as meek and unassuming, while they see themselves as adaptable and getting on with the practical task.

Sometimes Virgos can see themselves as helping while others see them as self martyring. Virgos tend to remain quiet while they are assimilating and understanding what others are saying. They are sometimes playful, and like to explore and investigate. They like to follow the details or follow the line of reasoning that leads to the generality. While Virgos are unassuming and non-egotistic, they can sometimes be gossipy, nosy, and nagging. They may appear to be passive-aggressive. Signs that lack the Virgo characteristics need to learn to discriminate, check out the details and ask pertinant questions.

7.7. LIBRA

Libra rules the kidneys, the lumbar region of the spine, the skin, and the ureters. Starting with Aries, we have moved around the Zodiac to the sign opposite Aries, which is Libra. While Arians are self-centred, Librans are other-centred. Librans find it very hard to be alone and need the companionship of others and of a partner. The symbol for Libra is the scales, so it is not surprising that Librans are known for weighing and balancing. The keyphrase for Libra is "I unite".

Like Aries and Cancer, Librans are initiating - they will take the first step and take action on something important to them. The action that Librans take may be to see the other person's viewpoint and compare and contrast it with their own. In this way, they take action in terms of thinking and speaking, but may find it hard to make a decision that leads to the type of action that Aries takes.

Librans, like Geminis, can be detached and appear a little aloof, while they are trying to be fair and objective. Others may want them to take their side, but Librans like to see the other person's point of view, and to balance or unite it with their own. John Lennon is a Libran and some of his work indicates the "I unite" keyphrase of Libra. Mahatma Ghandi was also a Libran, and he sought to bring independence to India in a harmonious and diplomatic way, and opposed all violence.

Librans tend to abstract and verbal, so they tend to unite ideas through words. Groucho Marx was famous for his clever words. "I would never join any club that was low enough to accept me as a member"! He also united many people through humour. Librans tend to do things harmoniously and diplomatically.

Librans are famous for seeing the other person's point of view. These people can be very beautiful and proportioned. They are children of Venus and like luxury and wealth. Julie Andrews, Brigitte Bardot, and Olivia Newton-John were all born under the sign of Libra. They are lovers of luxury and are attracted to wealth, jewellery and status. Because Librans can see the other person's point of view as well as their own, they can be indecisive. In fact, they are renowned for being indecisive!

Librans are diplomatic. They are tactful, impartial gracious and democratic. They can sometimes be seen by others as manipulative, vain and superficial, cowardly and people-pleasers. They can also be seen as being afraid of rejection.

7.8. SCORPIO

The bladder, the sigmoid flexure, prostate gland, pubic bone, the haemoglobin, and the nasal bones are also under the rule of Scorpio. Scorpio has two symbols, the scorpion or the snake, and the eagle. In the ancient wisdom, the snake has great wisdom, even knowledge of life and death, symbolised by its sloughing off its old skin and being reborn anew. The eagle too, may be associated with the Phoenix, which dies and is born again from the ashes. Both of these symbols, the snake and the eagle, are associated with secret wisdom and knowledge of life and death.

♏

Scorpio is a fixed sign like Taurus, Leo and Aquarius. That means that Scorpios can be steadfast and strong-willed in what they do, say and think. They can maintain their position. Ex-British Prime Minister Margaret Thatcher has her ascendant in Scorpio.

Like Cancer and Pisces, Scorpio is a water sign. Cancer symbolises the shallow water, such as that near the seashore. Pisces refers to the ocean. And Scorpio refers to the deep water of lakes and perhaps wells. Scorpio delves deep below the surface and plummets the depths. Scorpios can make good psychiatrists and psychologists, detectives and scientists.

Scorpios are believed to have piercing, hypnotic gazes and appear to see the truth hidden within the person. Such a person is almost always a Scorpio! Scorpios can have great power because of their understanding of other people and they can greatly influence others with this knowledge.

While Scorpios are often caring, nurturing and sensitive, they can sometimes be cruel. Scorpios are transformative and reforming. They can be devoted partners and followers. They are insightful because they can feel the truth hidden deep within others. They are often psychic in that they can receive feelings from super-sensory sources. Scorpio is sometimes called the "Sex sign" because Scorpios are deep and passionate in love.

7.9. SAGITTARIUS

Sagittarius rules the region of the body surrounding the hips, the sacral region of the spine, the coccygeal vertebrae, the femur, the ileum, the iliac arteries, the sciatic nerves, and the ischium. The symbol for Sagittarius is the centaur - the half-man, half-half. Some centaurs were wild and rough, while others overcame their animal nature and became refined and wise. The centaur Chiron taught the Greek heroes their skills and knowledge, including hunting, battle, surgery, philosophy, music and mathematics.

♐

The keyphrase for Sagittarius is "I seek". All Sagittarians strive to rise higher, for some it is social climbing and for others the seeking of knowledge and enlightenment. Like Gemini, Virgo and Pisces, Sagittarians are (or can be) highly adaptable and fit into situations which might challenge others. They are restless and want to be in action, whether mental or physical, seeking the higher things in life. They are ones who synthesise and draw conclusions and generalities from their experience.

Like Aries and Leo they are rules by enthusiastic passion rather than logic, practicality or emotions. They are passionate in what they do and they are direct in what they save, do and think. Sagittarians are social and seek to teach the world the knowledge and wisdom they have accumulated. For this reason they can sometimes be arrogant and "big mouthed".

Sagittarians value their independence, and seek to inspire others with their knowledge and optimism. Although some appear arrogant and tactless (because they are direct), they are often reasonable and listen to what others have to say. They are a happy lot who encourage and teach others the higher levels of knowledge. Sagittarians are generous and wise, philosophical and honest., They enthusiastically share the knowledge they have. They are original in their thinking and behaviour and curious about the universal nature of life and existence. They are frank and rather transparent (like Aries and Leo) but as they are honest, this isn't too important. They have few secrets.

Sagittarians are impartial. In this they are not cold or detached, but can passionately understand what motivates and drives others. They are prophetic and intuitive in the sense that enthusiasms decend upon them and reveal universal truths. Some Sagittarians are extremely tactless and exaggerating. They can be fanatical and even manic. Nero was a Sagittarian.

7.10. CAPRICORN

Capricorn rules the nees, skin, skeleton. Capricorns are prudent and reserved. The symbol for Capricorn is the sea goat. The word Capricorn comes from the Latin word for goat horn. While this also related to the cornucopia—

horn of plenty—and while Capricorn is associated with wealth, the wealth does not come magically—it comes from hard work or from knowledge. The fish tail associates Capricorn with water, and indicates that Capricorns are sensitive, although they may not show it.

♑

Capricorn is the sign of the head of business. Howard Hughes, Aristotle Onassis, and John Delorean were born Capricorns. Like Aries, Cancer, and Libra, Capricorn is an initiating sign. Capricorns, while cautious and prudent, do take action for practical and important reasons. They do not dive in, as Aries might; they carefully think about the practicalities and usefulness of what they do.

Capricorns are ambitious. They are responsible and goal oriented and they achieve their results through personl discipline and commitment. They are honorable and serious in what they do. Being extremely practical, they are well organised and can organise others. Capricorns are very professional and they can wait for the results of their efforts. Capricorns can be idealistic in a practical or useful way. Martin Luther King was born under Capricorn. They can be cold, heartless and selfish. Al Capone was born under Capricorn.

7.11. AQUARIUS

Aquarius rules the lower limbs and ankles. The characteristics of Aquarians is that they are said to be indifferent and unconventional. "Indifferent" is a keyword that suggests they tend not to show their emotions. And Aquarians are expected to be unoconventional in some way. The keyphrase of Aquarius is "I know". The symbol for Aquarius is sometimes thought of as the rippling waves on water, or as electromagnetic radiation.

♒

Aquarians tend to be fixed and constant in their thinking, and they are therefore strong-willed and persevering and steadfast in their beliefs, even if these beliefs are unconventional. Aquarians tend to appear to be detatched, and avoid showing their emotions. They tend to think in an abstract way, and rely on words and vision rather than on emotional sensitivity.

They like to be involved with people, and adopt an adult viewpoint. They are concerned with universal truths, or with generalities. Aquarians are charismatic and inventive. Many inventers are under the influence of Aquarius. Charles Darwin had his Sun in Aquarius as did Thomas Edison and Galileo.

Aquarians are idealistic and humanitarian. They are socially conscious, liberal and tolerant, and may be activists. They are modern and interested in all new ideas. Aquarians can be rebellious, anarchistic and may seem bizarre. They can be fanatics. Sometimes they appear to spacey, impractical do-gooders.

7.12. PISCES

Pisces rules the feet, the toes, and the fibrin of the blood. Pisceans are impressionable and inspirational. They are those who are born into a sign that is out of this world, and they often have difficulty coping with worldly life. The symbol is two fishes swimming in opposite directions tied together with a rope, or, in other versions, by their tales. The keyphrase of Pisces is "I believe".

♓

Pisces is like Gemini, Virgo and Sagittarius, in that it is a restless, adaptable and synthesising sign. Pisceans are often caring, sensitive and nurturing people who make good counsellors. In this, they are like Cancer and Scorpio. Roberto Assagioli had his Sun in Pisces. Pisces is an outward directed sign, and Pisces are mature other-concerned people. They are concerned with universal emotions and are psychic. Edgar Cayce was a Piscean.

They are open, loving and warm people who show compassion. They are often artistic and have a sense of rhythm, both in dance and language. Pisceans are visionary and creative. David Livingstone and Albert Einstein were both Pisceans. Pisceans can be susceptible to addiction. Aleister Crowley had his Moon in Pisces.

8

SPIRITUAL ASTROLOGY

Spiritual Astrology acquired this term to distinguish it from regular Astrology which, at the time of origination of this term, was striving to get acknowledged by the scientific fraternity as a science. Because of this, a form of astrology was unfolding that gave strict and inflexible interpretations for traditional aspects, etc. Those wishing to avoid the pitfalls of this pathway, and who may have wished to practice astrology from a different philosophical perspective, chose to distinguish between their astrological practise and that of the mainstream of astrology.

Furthermore, because of the need to obtain scientific credibility, it was decided that astrology should no longer have any identification with certain philosophical/ spiritual beliefs/or ideas especially Karma and Reincarnation as these concepts are unacceptable to many scientists. Accordingly, Spiritual Astrology does include, and we might even say specialises in, Karmic Astrology—including considerations of past-lives.

The concept of karma is readily acknowledged as being retrogressive, yet it also carries the certainty that what we do now will affect our future lives. So it is that the Law of Karma goes hand-in-hand with the Law of

Opportunity. Therefore, it is that being born into a specific Sun Sign (perhaps commonly known as birth sign - e.g. if you're born on the 6th June then you are a Gemini) carries a certain karma, as there are specific spiritual qualities that the soul is wishing to acquire during this current incarnation that are indicated by the Sun Sign.

Such an approach places the astrological information into a different range of contexts that derive their meaning from spiritual knowledge (also known as the Ancient Wisdom teachings) and the reading has far more to do with matters of the soul and spirit than with personality characteristics or fortune-telling.

Astrology was one of the Sacred Sciences in the ancient times, practised by priests and initiates of old. Astrology also allows us to gain an objective perspective on matters in our lives. Despite what we think of ourselves or what others say regarding ourselves, our charts tell us the truth if only we have eyes to see. For instance, there are branches of astrology concerned with the future and one such is called Progressions. The most common form of astrological progressions are termed Secondary Progressions whereby each day after birth is equal to one year of our life. Philosophically, we can see that this could make sense when we ponder that we spend nine months in the womb and the remaining three months would equal over 90 years in Secondary Progressions!

One cycle that each of us faces is that of the Progressed New Moon. For over three years prior to this event, and for some 3-4 years afterwards, we can be in a period of darkness. The past cycle has gone, we can no longer feel any life in our past and the future hasn't yet arrived. When a person is undergoing such a period in their lives it can be a tremendous help to understand that this isn't anything to do with their outer lives but, rather, a Cycle that they are experiencing. This can bring objectivity to the situation where otherwise the person might blame outer circumstances. Feeling that the past has gone, whilst also feeling in limbo, etc, they might take it that their marriage/relationship is over and so decide to end it when that might not be the actual case.

Astrology can thus be a great tool in self-knowledge and also help us in our relationships by providing us with understanding of how the other individuals really are. For instance, understanding the (astrological) inclinations of our children can help us to provide them with the unique help that they require as an individual. It can also absolve us of any feelings of inadequacy if people look to us accusingly because our child isn't 'normal'. The child's chart might indicate that they'd be the way they are no matter who their parents were!

Another aspect, otherwise denied by regular astrology, features the possibility of contacting the spiritual guide of the client—who really knows the main landmarks of this incarnation—either to indicate the particular path and give advice or for the astrologer to act as a messenger to bring a specific message from the guide to the client.

9

KARMIC ASTROLOGY

Karmic astrology is not a new astrology, "another" astrology. It is the spiritual evolution fruit of a society—rediscovering—reincarnation concept, occulted for such a long time. Traditional astrology limits itself to an approach of the outside personality and too often pass next to the essential keys for the understanding of the individual. Karmic astrology happens to be therapeutic because—the psychoanalysis enables us to understand it—many problems are the result of a dissension between conscious and unconscious.

Karmic astrology is a very rigorous tool permitting us to understand events. Very often, the karmic indications of the chart are confirmed by more psychic approaches such as channeling or regression. The fact is astrology confirms these approaches giving the same indications but by another means, prove indeed previous lives do exist, and one can recover their traces. Astrology will have a more scientific approach permitting to judge if these reminiscences brought by channeling are real.

Your astrology chart is a picture of your inner person, in the same sense that your physical body is a picture of your outer person. Your chart is set (or 'predestined') in the same way that your body is set (or 'predestined') at the moment of your birth. Your physical body remains essentially the same throughout your lifetime, even as it grows and matures and changes. Your inner self remains essentially the same, too, in spite of life lessons that make us grow and mature and change along the way. It's easy enough to see the physical changes in our body; all we have to do is look in a mirror. We aren't as aware of the changes taking place in our emotional, intellectual and spiritual bodies, because they're invisible, and are only reflected in the way we live our lives.

Contrary to popular belief, there's nothing "new age" about astrology; the basic tenets have remained unchanged - except for the addition of a newfound planet or two - for thousands of years, literally speaking. Before we look at the ways we used our natal birth chart to plan our present life personality, let's do a quick review of the basic components astrologers use to interpret an individual's birth chart.

The science of astrology is a science of influence. Each of the planets in our solar system, along with the Sun and the Moon, has a specific influence on our planet (Earth) and on those who inhabit it. There are ten planets in all, and all ten planets appear in every person's birth chart.

There are also ten primary urges that we all experience just by being human beings. We work with those ten urges as we're planning (in between lives) what lessons we want to learn while we're here. We should think of these urges as the desire to experience a unique and specific energy that will support our life lessons.

Because the ten planets correspond with - and will therefore define our individual reaction to—these basic life urges, their position at the time of our birth will determine how we can use these urges to facilitate our growth by expressing ourselves and experiencing our life under the influence of the energy of the planet that represents each urge. A quick check of your natal chart will give you a good idea of where you placed your learning emphasis in this lifetime.

1. The Sun—The External Self
2. The Moon—The Emotional Foundation
3. Mercury—Communicating with Others
4. Venus—Self-Image
5. Mars—Assertiveness
6. Jupiter—Cultural Implications
7. Saturn—Your Place in the World
8. Uranus—Personal Freedom
9. Neptune—The Source of Happiness
10. Pluto—Mastery Over the Self

These same ten urges while in human form, no matter who we have chosen to be or what lessons we have come here to learn. The position of the planets in our charts, and the inter-relationship of each planet to the others, will determine how we use these urges to our advantage in accomplishing our soul growth objectives. In other words, the role we play is different for each of us, but the basic game of life is the same for all.

The planet defines the urge, but it's the astrological sign in which the planet is located at the moment of our birth that determines the specific challenge through which we've chosen to characterise the urge of the planet. There are twelve astrological signs, which correspond to the twelve constellations in our galaxy. As the planets orbit around the sun, they pass through the signs of the Zodiac; each sign modifies any planet it contains by filtering the planet's basic energy through it's own tones, setting the stage and coloring the scenery against which the story of your life will unfold.

By placing specific planets (which represent specific urges) within specific signs, you have planned your chart in such a way that the only path to personal fulfillment within a particular area of your life is to be expressing the urge the way you chose to express it in your birthchart. You are capable of expressing the urge in other ways (as we all are), but it's only by expressing the planetary urge within the boundaries you set (by choosing which sign to place it in) that you can find peace and contentment with yourself.

Let's say that part of your life plan requires you to work on the issue of self-worth, represented by the planet Venus. How are you going to challenge yourself? You have twelve signs to choose from, with each sign offering a completely different learning environment. If you choose Venus in Taurus, for example, you're giving yourself the opportunity to develop your sense of self-worth through a material and sensual process. If, on the other hand, you choose to position Venus in Gemini, you're planning to use social communication to accomplish the same goal.

A birth chart is divided into twelve houses which are mathematically calculated according to the time, date and place of your birth; each of your planets is located in one of the houses. As we develop our lifeplan, we use the house influence to determine which arena in life will be most beneficial to our life lessons when we experience the specific energy of the planet in the sign that supports it. For example, if we position Venus in the third house of our chart, we know that our lessons involving self-worth will be most noticeable to us on a conscious level when we're communicating with others, since communication is the third house arena.

In other words, the houses are the arena in the material world where we experience the consequences of the way we are handling the basic game depicted by the planet:

1. The first house represents your personality, your disposition, your health, your temperament, and your physical build and appearance. It provides a mirror image of the way you project yourself to the rest of the world, based on obvious external behavior.
2. The second house concerns itself with possessions of all kinds, and your attitude towards them. The essence of your material value system is reflected here.
3. The third house reflects your mind, and your mindset regarding your personal relationship with your environment and your immediate family. It is in this house that the way you express yourself in day to day life is made apparent.
4. The fourth house represents that part of your personal foundation which is based in the home, and can also reflect parental influences on your present moment self.
5. The fifth house reflects on your creativity and your ability (or inability) to instigate change. Affairs of the heart and intuitional issues are also brought to fruition here.
6. The sixth house focuses into your working relationships with other people, with an emphasis on the lesson of dealing with everyone on an equal basis, regardless of apparent, external status quo.
7. The seventh house provides insight into your close relationships, both personal and professional, and reflects the opportunities for positive interaction on a fair and balanced basis.

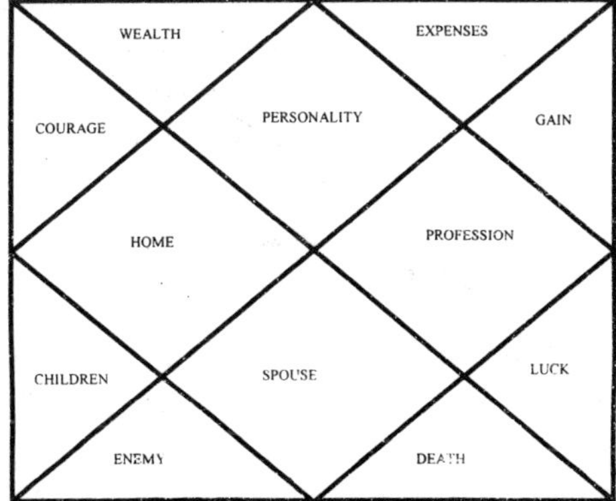

8. The eighth house represents possessions from outside sources (such as legacies and inheritances) and focuses into your personal value system regarding the issues of death and the afterlife.
9. The ninth house reflects your interest (or lack of interest) in higher education on all levels, including the philosophical issues related to your moral value system.
10. The tenth house deals with your aspirations, your ambitions, and your public status, and focuses into the people, events and circumstances that contribute to your personal image in the outside world.
11. The eleventh house deals with group interactions, with an emphasis on the way you interact in the more detached relationships that are a part of your everyday lifestyle.
12. The twelfth house reflects on the inner you, and your need for solitary moments in which you can balance your negative thoughts with more positive ones. In the extreme, this house can reflect a tendency towards escapism.

The bottom line in understanding how we use our natal birthchart to accommodate our lifeplanis simple: the planet represents one aspect of your personality during this lifetime, and the sign defines how that aspect will respond to life's challenges and opportunities in the life arena determined by which house the sign and planet are in at the moment of your birth.

9.1. ASTROLOGICAL BIRTH CHART

The meaning of an astrological chart is subject to interpretation, and there are many ways of interpreting astrological data. When we look at the information provided by our birth chart under the light of Universal Law, we can see that the concept of using astrological influences to support our life plan fits within the Universal Law parameters of each soul choosing their own path to spiritual evolvement. What better tool to support our growth than a vehicle that provides exactly the urges, in exactly the right environment, under the perfect conditions we need in which to grow spiritually?

Karmic astrology makes sense to our conscious minds, in a world that all too often doesn't. Astrological insight can provide rational, reasonable explanations for some of the things we do and say—especially the things we don't understand about ourselves—and it offers explanations for things that other people say and do to us that sometimes affect our lives dramatically yet leave us wondering (for years, sometimes) what happened, and why.

The karmic interpretation of our birth chart is based on the perspective of life and it's meaning as reflected in Universal Law. Each soul separates from the God-essence for the purpose of learning God's truth through it's own experiences. Lifetime after lifetime—as different kinds of people living in different cultures and different historical eras—we accumulate knowledge that confirms or denies God's universal truth. Here on the planet Earth, our emphasis is on learning experiences involving the emotional self.

We get a new "outside" body for each lifetime, but our "inside bodies"—our emotional, intellectual, and spiritual bodies—accumulate experience from lifetime to lifetime. We are born into this lifetime with all of our experiences—good and bad—in our subconscious mind. Our intention was to remain open to our subconscious memories so that we wouldn't waste our time and effort in this lifetime repeating lessons already learned. It doesn't work that way, of course; by the time we're old enough to talk, we've usually forgotten our subconscious mind even exists, and are back at square one living a conscious life in a physical world.

Just because we don't remember our gameplan doesn't mean that all of the people, events and circumstances that we worked into it don't show up, exactly when they're supposed to, to help us learn what we intended to learn. Working closely with other souls who were planning a lifetime in the same culture and the same historical era, we determined what problems we would encounter, what obstacles would block our path, and what golden opportunities would be presented. Each detail was carefully scrutinised and measured to provide the maximum growth opportunity for everyone involved.

It's human nature to ask a very obvious question: if we, as eternal entities, worked out all the details of our upcoming lives ahead of time, why is life so fraught with sadness, and pain, and frustration? Why are so many of our relationships rocky, and so many of the circumstances in our lives less than what we want them to be?

The answer is as obvious as the question: because we've lost contact with our subconscious mind, and we have no conscious memory of being a part of the planning process. If we did - if we opened up our subconscious mind - we'd recognise that all of our problems are familiar ones, of our own making. We, in our universal wisdom, put them into our life plan so that we could encounter them, resolve them, and learn from them, contributing to our human awareness of who we are and what it truly means to be happy. Working with only the conscious mind, we forget that we planned it all - we CHOSE this path to spiritual evolvement during this particular lifetime - and all too often we end up falling victim to the victim role itself.

9.1.1. Stressful Life

We chose the exact moment of our impending birth, knowing full well that the positioning of the planets within the astrological signs and houses of our birth chart would determine our psychological profile—a profile that would provide us with the strengths we need in the areas of our life where we would need them most so that our life lessons—as we ourselves defined them before we were born—could be learned without undue stress.

It looked great on the planning board, but stress—as we have all learned from experience—is a part of our everyday lives. Some of that stress comes from not understanding what's really going on in our lives and not having a clue as to why our relationships with other people are what they are. Without a conscious sense of the big picture (what lessons we're here to learn, and how those lessons will be presenting themselves) we often find ourselves wondering, "Why does this always happen to me?"

Our natal birth chart helps us remember the life plan we put together for ourselves by reminding us that we wanted to overcome this challenge in this lifetime, so we put this planet in this house, under this sign, so our life would be filled with situations that we have the opportunity to grow from. Knowing what lessons we intended to learn while we're here helps us put things in their proper perspective. Instead of feeling that our lives are chaotic, we can see the order of the universe reflected in the people, events and circumstances that make up our day to day lifestyle.

Whether we are consciously aware of the learning opportunities in our lives or not, they present themselves exactly the way we intended them to when we put our life plan together. Our life always goes in the direction we intended it to go, with or without our co-operation.

We can learn easy or we can learn hard, but, since the purpose of life is to learn, we will learn, one way or the other. The birth chart serves as our roadmap for this lifetime. It tells us where we need to go and shows us the fastest and easiest way to get there. Not having conscious awareness of the purpose of our lives is like traveling cross country without ever looking at the road atlas; sooner or later, we'll get where we're going, but we'll take the long way, hit a lot of unnecessary detours, and miss most of the great sites to see along the way, because we never realised they were there.

Once we recognise the curriculum we've set for ourselves in this lifetime—once we've consciously charted our course in life—we begin to notice that life isn't as stressful as it used to be. When we ask ourselves "Why does this always happen to me?" we have an answer - an answer that makes perfect sense. We recognise those people and events and circumstances for what they are: tools to help us look and listen to what's happening in our lives so we can grow spiritually. Co-operating with the curriculum, instead of fighting against it because we think "life shouldn't be like this" motivates us to change ourselves and/or our lifestyle so that we're living life the way we think it should be lived. Confident that we are doing what we're supposed to be doing in our lives, we live life to the fullest, understanding that the pleasure principle is our human birthright. We find the inner peace that everyone's always talking about when we find our own ability to interpret life's roadsigns and choose the right path for learning our life lessons in a positive way.

Life is an excellent teacher: what better way to remind ourselves that the decisions we're making, the way we're choosing to live our lives, and the person we've chosen to express to others are not what we intended them to be than have each of those decisions, each of those choices, and each of those interactions result in pain, frustration and happiness? The old adage, "If it doesn't feel good, it's not right," is totally appropriate for the karmic learning experience in which friction is intended to spark awareness of who we are, what we believe in, and how we express those beliefs on a daily basis.

Our subconscious memory is fully aware of the life we planned to live and the lessons we intended to learn. We know instinctively the directions we should be moving in if we want to accomplish our purpose in being here. The better we understand our life plan, as documented in our natal birth chart, the better we get at making life choices that help us express that purpose in the way we live our lives. Life gets better, and so do we.

One of the catch phrases in our society today is "body, mind and spirit." The last few decades have seen a resurgence of interest in "the complete person"—an important move away from the days when doctors dealt with the physical body, teachers and psychiatrists dealt with the intellectual body, and preachers dealt with the spiritual body. One of our purposes in life is to learn to integrate these three aspects of ourselves—aspects which, when balanced and integrated into a whole, make us look, think and feel like a complete person. Each of these elements is a necessary and equal part of our life plan.

It's easy to understand why some people consider the physical body to be more important than the mind or the spirit—after all, most people think of our body as "who we are." When we describe ourselves to others, it's usually in physical terms, and—we think—without our bodies to keep them in, the mind and soul couldn't exist. This misunderstanding leads many of us to putting too much emphasis on the physical aspects of our lives; we judge ourselves and often others by the way we look, whether other people find us attractive, and whether or not we are "beautiful people" in the physical sense of the world.

We chose our physical body—in the same way that we chose our psychological profile—before we came into this lifetime. It changes our whole perspective when we realise that we look the way we look, and others see us the way they see us—whether their perception is valid or not—because we gave ourselves the physical body that we thought would be most useful in learning the lessons we came in to learn. It's a given that the way we choose to look in this lifetime brings home the universal lessons of recognising the importance—or unimportance, as the case may be—of our physical body in relating with others, and makes it obvious to everyone how we rate our physical self against our spiritual and intellectual bodies.

Everyone who comes to life on this physical plane has the shared lesson of integrating the aspects of our life triad—our bodies, minds and spirits—so that spirit is the true decision maker in our lives and we think, feel, and act as one integrated person, instead of having a "physical personality," an "intellectual personality," and a "spiritual personality," which we often only share with others at church gatherings. For some of us, our physical body makes our lives easier, and for some of us, looking the way we do makes life difficult. Whatever the case may be, we can rest confident that we chose what we thought would be the perfect body to accomplish our life lessons in. Because it was a part of our life plan, our body is perfect for our own purposes.

The body—which constitutes one-third of our being in a physical lifetime—is a temporary, short-term home that provides us with the physical senses, physical needs and physical desires that catalyst our growth through interaction with others and sends an unspoken message about who we are just by the way other people perceive us. The second third of our life triad is the mind, or the intellect. We all know that our minds accumulate our understanding of life as we perceive it throughout our lifetime; like the physical body, it's a learning tool in it's own right.

We can use our minds to reach out to one another and to the collective consciousness. Through the mind, we can watch, look and listen to what is happening in our world, analyse the people and events and circumstances that make up that world, and come to know our own truth through the process. It's the mind that decides what is good for us and what is not, and the mind which calls our conscious priorities in life.

Communication is key to insight; the mind gives us the ability to communicate on all levels as much as we need to until we reach the position in our growth process where we truly understand that no man (or woman) is an island. It is the conscious mind that comes to the realisation that life works better—for us and for everyone else—when it's a shared experience.

We chose the people we'd be sharing those experiences with, too. It was us who decided - in agreement with the other souls - who we would run into in this lifetime, and the roles we'd play in each other's lives, all to accommodate lessons some of us needed to learn and some of us needed to teach. The impact of our intellectual body becomes almost frightening when we stop rushing through our lives long enough to realise that we have an impact - large or small - on every person we come in contact with, every minute of every day of our life. A passing comment that seemed insignificant in our life plan may be the catalyst for major change in the life plan of the person we made that comment to. Through our minds, we are all interconnected through the universal consciousness; for better or for worse, our thoughts, our words and our actions affect those we are sharing our lives with.

The mind's natural ability to absorb information allows us to explore a vast array of religious and philosophical perspectives, sort through them intelligently, and draw our own conclusions about what is true for us and what is not. It is the mind that gives us the intellectual ability to decide for ourselves what our values in life will be, along with the communication skills required to share those values with others. The mind is our gateway to the universal truths we came here to understand, and intellect demands that we understand the "why" as well as we understand the "wherefore." Because we are intelligent beings, we don't have to accept anything at face value.

The final third of our life triad is the soul, or spirit. Our soul—like God—is infinite; it is the part of us that goes on and on forever, accumulating knowledge from every lifetime that we live, on every level of existence, but always remaining a part of the God-consciousness. Our life lessons—and the experiences through which we learn them - change our perceptions of truth, but they don't change who we really are; our soul essence is the determining force behind whom and who we need to be and do in any given lifetime in our continual quest for God-like perfection.

Your birthchart reminds you of the way your soul wanted life to be in this lifetime; it defines precisely the path you need to follow if you want to learn what you intended to learn and teach what you intended to teach by being the individual you said you would be, playing the role(s) you intended to play. The Sun is considered a "current life experience" planet because, like the physical body itself, the data applies only to this lifetime, and is not carried forward.

We chose the personality traits we chose because we felt, in our universal wisdom, that they would be exactly the traits we needed in order to accomplish our soul-growth purpose. In this sense, our decision to be born under the influence of a particular Sun sign was a decision based on a need to integrate into our current life experience the mindset that would be most appropriate to our goals, and the external personality traits that would allow us to express ourselves in a way that will support what we are trying to accomplish.

The other nine planets have more of an inner impact than an outward expression, and deal primarily with our "sub-personalities"—the emotions and the will. Emphasis here is placed on the inner drives and motivations that silently direct the manifestation of the external traits that we have chosen. Each section of the Profile will deal specifically with the planet at hand, and look at the impact of that planet on your external self (that is, how you express the energies of that planet in that sign, both positively and negatively) and the inner self (how those energies influence you and the choices you make.)

Our sub-personalities - defined as our emotional motivations for the way we choose to express ourselves in any given situation - play havoc with our sense of peace and serenity, for it is these "different sides of ourselves" that seem to be in constant conflict with each other, and leave us in a state of inner turmoil.

One side of us may want to have fun all the time, while another side feels that we must work hard to accomplish our goals. One side may seem very positive about a particular situation, while another side looks at it with a negative view. Because these sub-personalities work simultaneously, we end up feeling confused and unsure of how to proceed, and too often end up not proceeding at all.

Most people remain in a state of "personal unawareness" until the emotional pain and confusion becomes unbearable, and they must make changes, in themselves and in their lives, if they are ever going to be at peace. The difference is, literally, "personal transformation." You haven't really changed; you've just reorganised, and taken control of your life back from these emotional sub-personalities that have been driving you and controlling your life in the process. These sides can cause confusion and misery once they've gained control, because we don't recognise them as sub-personalities, and they feel just like the "real" us.

Part of the life process in this level of existence is learning to integrate all of those parts of our personalities into one "core personality self." This inner self deals with life—and the circumstances, events and people that comprise it—from an objective and impartial foundation, without letting the emotional selves take over and create crisis and conflict where it is not appropriate.

As you open yourself up to the idea of personal awareness, you should realise that these sub-personalities will inevitably surface more and more often, in an effort to draw your attention to them and let you work your way through the process of integrating them into the whole. Any aspect that you might forget will certainly surface as you go through this transformation process. In a sense, it is the dark before the storm, and it doesn't feel like life is getting any better at all. In fact, it may feel like you're moving backwards, and getting lost in your own emotions.

Your emotional selves will be expressing themselves more than ever before, and you will be much more aware of what is happening. You will come to understand that this is a natural part of the learning process, and will recognise that you are experiencing heightened emotions so that you will know what sub-personalities you are dealing with, and can bring those aspects back into balance with your core personality self.

It's easy to get confused about "who we are" when all of the "parts of our personalities" are claiming to be "the real me." Anytime we allow one of these emotional aspects to take over, we are looking at the world around us through this purely emotional perspective, and our reactions and decisions are based on invalid emotional information instead of an objective evaluation of what is really happening. Our purpose is to expose these sub-personalities—these inner fears and hidden motivations—that are affecting your life on a daily basis. With this new perspective, we hope you will reclaim the priority position of your core personality, which is the only "real you."

As you begin to see what is "real" in yourself and what is emotionally driven, you will find that your entire perspective on life—and on other people—changes drastically.

It is important that you understand that these sub-personalities are NOT real. They have been created by lifetimes of emotional experiences, and they are simply an illusion. Think of these emotional drives as a display in a holography exhibit: a three dimensional hologram of a woman dancing looks solid. It seems to move as you walk around it, but, if you try to touch it, it isn't there after all. Your hand goes out, and finds only empty space.

Sub-personalities are no more solid than a hologram, even those sub-personalities that make you feel the most anxious, the most guilty, the most angry. They represent, quite simply, habitual patterns of the brain, in the same way that the hologram represents patterns of light focused on film.

As you study your Inner Profile, try to recognise which sub-personalities are influencing your decisions.

You will find that each sub-personality has it's own characteristics, and represents your set way of thinking or feeling that has become so familiar to you that you don't even think of it as a response; it is automatic. The ones you are most likely to find controlling where they shouldn't be are anger, resentment, jealousy, fear, selfishness, or prejudice. Remember that the sub-personality in control at any given moment is determining how you think and relate to the world - and you will find that this view is often very distorted from your own perspective, without the sub-personality's influence.

These sub-personalities are not a negative influence in your life, unless you allow them to take control. All of them are trying to help you; all of them are "about" protecting you from being hurt, or disappointed, or embarrassed.

When you give control of your life over to these sub-personalities, they assert themselves even more, in an ever-growing effort to provide you with "walls against the world," walls built on negative emotions which, in your self-defensive state, you feel justified to feel: angry, hurt, sullen, jealous, or guilty. This negative energy naturally distances you from any situation that might put you at emotional risk, and presents a major obstacle to the open and honest relationship with the world you must establish in order to find real happiness.

Your Higher Self is your core personality essence that has always been you , is you in this current life experience, and will continue to be you in lifetime after lifetime after lifetime. As you learn to respond from this inner core instead of from the sub-personalities, you will find a new sense of harmony in your life.

You will feel as though you can finally get past all the little ghosts and gremlins that have bullied and threatened you since you were a child. What we are all seeking in this lifetime is an experience of oneness, of feeling contented within ourselves. We believe that the first step toward that objective is an acknowledgment of the key role these sub-personalities play in your life, and an honest evaluation of whether you are controlling them or they are controlling you.

10

PREDICTIVE ASTROLOGY

When undertaking to forecast using astrology, secondary progressions is the best starting point. Since the natal patterns must be considered to properly assess the progressed chart, it is impossible to overlook the birth potential, an essential element in predicting. The relatively few exact aspects formed between the progressed and natal planets offer a background theme or the main plot to a story. Several similar configurations, by aspect and planetary natures, indicate the prominent theme for any time period. The contacts also show how an individual is maturing and making use of his or her birth potential. For these reasons, the progressed patterns also provide an excellent guideline for interpreting activity shown in the Solar and Lunar Returns falling within the same time frame.

A few consequential rules must be applied when judging the progressions. The first of these is that the orbit of aspect must be kept very tight. In progressions, the planets move very slowly from their birth position, and some of the outer planets will hardly move at all over an entire lifetime. The calculation for the progressed planets is that one year in the life of an individual is equal to one day of planetary movement. So, for someone aged 30, the progressed planets will be at the sign and degree they held on the 30th day following birth. The Ascendant and Midheaven will also progress about a degree per year in a counter-clockwise position. Use of a computer program is recommended to calculate the progressed chart.

The active orbit of aspect is 1 degree for any planet or angle, and 1.5 degrees for the Sun and Moon, or the Lights. The Lights are given a bit more width because they are instrumental in so many personal areas of life. Since the Sun progresses at the rate of about a degree per year, this means that when it moves within range to aspect another planet, the aspect will be active for about three years. This is 1.5 years (or 1.5 degrees) approaching the exact aspect and 1.5 years moving away from exact. When a progressing planet approaches an aspect to the natal Sun, the aspect will be active for the duration of the time that the planet is within that 1.5 degree range. The length of time the aspect is active depends upon the speed of the specific planet.

The progressing Moon moves approximately one degree per month, depending upon its speed at birth, so the aspects it forms will be felt for about three months. For the remaining planets, the time period of an active orbit depends on the varying rates of speed in which they are progressing. Some aspects involving the outer planets will remain active for months or years at a time, and must always be considered in light of other indicators for the time period in question. Although within the proper orb, some of these long-term aspects remain dormant unless stimulated by transits, or emphasised by similar progressions.

While noting the active aspects, they should be listed by priority. Angular contacts are given top billing, and these include several possible combinations. Aspects formed between the natal or progressed Ascendant with natal or progressed planets or Lights fall in this group, as well as the natal or progressed Midheaven with natal or progressed planets or Lights. These types of contacts signify important and eventful periods. These links will always be found when an important life event takes place. In fact, it is safe to assume that without such contacts, the time period is likely to remain rather routine. The more angles that become involved in aspects with the planets, the more significant the time period becomes for changes and for events to take place. The types of events represented by an active Midheaven do not differ greatly from those reflected by an active Ascendant, with the exnception that the Ascendant is slightly more influential in health issues.

Due to this similarity, it is best to judge the qualities of the planet and the aspect it makes to an angle. The Midheaven can be considered as slightly Solar in nature and the Ascendant as Lunar in nature, but events linked to either are quite personal, frequently regarded as rather major turning points by the individual. Of the aspects, the conjunction, opposition and square are the most potent.

Before exploring the various planetary potentials, the remainder of the contacts should be noted. Following the angular aspects in priority are those made by the Sun. Once again, the Sun will usually be involved in one or more active aspect at times of climactic life events, and this may be either the natal or the progressed Sun. When both the angles and the Sun are involved in aspects, it is predictive of major life events unfolding. The more activity, the more profound the events will be. The nature of the planet involved in a contact with the Sun or angle provides insight to the types of events coming due.

When the Sun, either progressing or natal, becomes involved in an aspect with an angle, a momentous time period is underway and the most significant events of life are shown in these contacts. For instance, marriage will often take place with these Sun/angle aspects, this being more frequent in a woman's chart. The hard aspects, such as the conjunction, square or opposition are usually more significant for eventful times than the softer sextile and trine. It is beneficial to also consider the minor aspects when they are near exact.

The ruler of the natal Ascendant should next be considered for active aspects, either natal or progressed. Take into consideration the natal prominence of each planet when prioritising the remaining contacts. If a natal planet is positioned on an angle, most elevated, leader or part of a stellium, or in some way outstanding in the chart, the aspects it forms will be more dominant in the theme that begins to reveal itself. The aspects of the Moon are very important, especially those made by progressing planets to the natal Moon. The aspects made by the progressing Moon also mark off important personal events. However, since it moves so quickly, this Moon is quite temporal in nature, thus these contacts must be considered in light of the remaining active aspects. Nevertheless, it will usually be making an exact aspect to a planet that quite appropriately describes even a relatively minor event.

Once all of the active aspects have been noted, it is not difficult to arrive at a general theme suggested by the type of contacts and the planets involved in the aspects. For an important event to take place there must be a minimum of three similar aspects or configurations which suggest such an event. For very profound or life altering events, this number usually increases markedly and is often heavily stimulated by similar transiting configurations at the time such an event takes place.

In noting the active aspects, note also the house ruled by the planets involved in aspects. Events corresponding with the houses will take place when the ruler of a house becomes involved in activity. This rule works in reverse as well. For instance, marriage will not take place unless the ruler of the marriage house is active in the progressions.

In judging the theme within the progressed chart, it is most helpful to keep in mind the traditional meanings of the planets and the aspects. Mars, Saturn, Uranus and Pluto are more apt to tell of reversals when involved in harsh aspects than planets such as Venus or Jupiter. Generally, squares are more difficult than trines when judging the way events will materialise on an earthly level. This is not a hard and fast rule, however, and the following must be considered:

When planets that were in aspect in the natal chart are once again linked together through progressed aspects, they foretell of potentially important events to take place. The type of aspect does not matter, only that the two are once more linked together. At times of very significant events there will frequently be several of these repeating links made in the progressions.

There will always be potential for the birth aspect to predominate, no matter what new aspect is formed between the two. This means that an easy aspect in the birth chart should not cause undue problems when it forms a stressful aspect. It also means that a harsh aspect in the birth chart should always be considered for the type of stress signified when preparing for an easier aspect among the same two planets in the progressions. The nature of the planet as well as the nature of the aspect must be considered, and each aspect must be considered alongside all of the other indicators in the progressed chart for the time in question. To reiterate, for any important event to transpire either for good or ill, there must be at least three similar aspects that describe the event.

By judging all of the progressed contacts, a theme will appear and then it is time to account for the transiting planets. The transits provide excellent testimony for events that correspond with the main theme in the progressions. They are also exceptional as timing devices. A transiting planet is more potent when stimulating progressed aspects than if only contacting a natal planet. Unless the transit stimulates activity showing in the progressions, a transit may go by with hardly any notice whatsoever. The easiest way to tabulate all of the activity occurring in the progressions and transits is to use a three wheel chart with the natal chart in the center, the progressed chart in the middle ring, and the transiting planets on the outside wheel.

The major transiting planets are the most important element in prediction, and these reflect every significant event an individual becomes involved in.

The Sun and Mars are used as timers, and it will be when they swing into a pattern with the outer transiting planets to stimulate the progressions that events will take place.

In judging the important transits, look for contacts among the transiting planets that repeat a theme or pattern showing in the progressed chart. The transiting planets involved in these duplicate configurations will also stimulate the progressed chart patterns at critical times. The more important events will be reflected in several of these transiting significators.

Although the allowable orbit can be much wider for transiting contacts, at the precise time of important events, there will be one or more exact aspect between a transiting planet to the progressed configuration. The planet(s) making this exact contact will very accurately describe the current event.

When the progressed aspects tell a story, and then the transiting planets repeat that story, it is safe to predict a certain trend and certain types of events. Use the faster moving planets to time the event. The Sun and/or Mars will usually be found on an angle of the natal or progressed chart, or stimulating a prominent configuration within the progressions when the event takes place. At the time the event takes place, the transiting planets will also be making contacts among themselves that repeat links found earlier!

When the progressed aspects tell a story, and then the transiting planets repeat that story, it is safe to predict a certain trend and certain types of events. Use the faster moving planets to time the event. The Sun and/or Mars will usually be found on an angle of the natal or progressed chart, or stimulating a prominent configuration within the progressions when the event takes place. At the time the event takes place, the transiting planets will also be making contacts among themselves that repeat links found earlier!

So, the most important times will be when the angles are stimulated, the Sun is involved in aspects, and progressed aspects reconnect planets that were in aspect in the nativity. At the same time, the major transiting planets will emphasise and stimulate these progressed configurations, while making similar contacts among themselves. Finally, the transits of the Sun and Mars will time the event.

When a planet becomes prominent in the progressed chart through an angular position or through its involvement in several active aspects, an assessment of its inherent qualities will outline the probable events it relates to. To get a clearer idea of the planetary potential, consider the natal aspects along with the nature of the planet. This is true for both progressed aspects and aspects made by transiting planets.

Unless they are extremely afflicted in the nativity, the Sun, Venus, and Jupiter can generally be anticipated to reflect fortunate times. All three of these may signify material benefits and pleasant occassions. The Sun and Jupiter signify events involving honor, and benefactors. One is often in a position to make progress through associations with those of honor or high standing in the community.

Jupiter tells of material or spiritual wealth, and when it is harmoniously aspecting the Midheaven, it reflects upon professional opportunities and recognition. If in aspect to the Ascendant, it shows opportunities more personal in nature. Both Venus and Jupiter signify social trends and ceremonies. When they are in a harmonious aspect with each other, they often signify elite social affairs or meeting a wealthy mate. Venus is often prominent during pleasant events such as childbirth, marriage, and similar happy occasions. These three can be considered the benefics.

There are some warnings to heed if these planets become involved in numerous harsh aspects, especially involving the angles. At those times they can signify illness, grief, loss and so forth, if combined with several similar configurations. Keep in mind that a benefic on an angle indicates harmony and ease. Countering aspects to such a benefic from a planet with an opposing nature reflects upon circumstances that will interfere with this harmony. Thus they often signify "disease" or disease. When the benefic is angular and in conflict with another benefic, with other indications in agreement, the prevalent indication is one of loss or grief.

The Sun rules the father and the husband in a female chart, and the aspects made to it reflect either a time of ease or of hardship for those people. Mars is also an indicator of masculine affairs, and co-rules a woman's husband or male children.

Venus is similar in a man's chart, as it reflects events involving his wife. The Moon signifies the mother for everyone and must be considered as a secondary indicator of a man's wife. The Moon becomes prominent when events involving motherhood, or women's interests are arriving. Venus with the Moon suggests things feminine and lacy; a bridal shower for instance. The Moon is also reflective of public opinion. It accurately reflects times of personal popularity and support as well as times of reversal in this respect.

Mars and Saturn are often deemed the malefics. Uranus and Pluto also have certain attributes that will frequently find them on this list. However, just as the benefic planets sometimes correspond with unfortunate events, these potentially problematic planets are often prominent at times of great success. The potential of any planet can generally be found by assessing the remaining active aspects at the time it comes into prominence. "The majority rules", so to speak. If the majority of the active aspects are fortunate, then one or two stressful aspects is nothing to be alarmed about. It will likely reflect upon the overcoming of a barrier, which allows for much progress and happiness.

The natal condition of a planet must always be considered, and when a particular planet becomes prominent, look to its house rulership for the department of life reflected upon. This becomes more important when one planet is harshly aspected by several progressed and transiting planets at the same time. The area of life ruled by such a planet should be addressed for weaknesses and adjustment.

Mars and Pluto hold some qualities in common. Both reflect upon new ventures, initiative and taking control. Both can signify confrontations, forceful circumstances, and even tragedy, depending on the overall chart indications. These two in conflicting aspect with each other can reflect great danger, especially if other indications agree or if they held a conflicting relationship in the natal chart.

Saturn and/or Pluto will most often be in harsh aspect to the Sun at times of ill health since the Sun rules the vitality. These health indicators involving the Sun often point to hereditary conditions, while those involving the Moon show functional problems. The most often found aspect reflecting a functional problem is Mars in stressful contact with the Moon. Mars or Pluto in harsh aspect to the Moon can indicate upheaval within the home, the mother's ill health or forceful issues involving a woman.

Uranus signifies a new era, and temporary associations with those who can act as a catalyst to new experience. It can also be a sign of extreme and sudden disruption to existing circumstances if involved inharmoniously with other planets or points.

Saturn signifies authorities and older people, as well as issues involving the professional status. One of the best aspects Saturn can make is a sextile or trine to the progressed Moon. This reflects a time of great achievement at a professional and personal level. It frequently signifies fortunate real estate dealings, as well. Some of the most unfortunate times coincide with harsh aspects from transiting Saturn or Uranus to the progressed Sun or Moon. These often indicate hard times and heavy losses with Saturn, and great upsets and potentially scandalous events with Uranus.

Mercury and Neptune are neutral. Mercury will frequently take on characteristics associated with the planet it most closely aspects. It can be counted on to signify intellectual concerns, movement, agreements, and communications of all sorts. It is usually involved in angular aspects when a name change takes place or when one's name becomes prominent, such as connections with the media. Frequently, it reflects affairs involving minor children.

Neptune's nature is to eliminate boundaries, and this it does even in its manner of manifesting when active. It is difficult to curb it into a precise category. On one hand it reflects confusing issues, deceptions, intrigue, and escapist tendencies. On the other hand it reflects true inspiration and having dreams become a reality. If strong in the natal chart, Neptune may reflect upon true prophetic visions when coming to a prominent aspect in the progressed chart. In any case, it suggests that old conditions are dissolving while new entanglements are forming. Neptune must be judged in accordance with its natal prominence and condition, as well as the rest of the progressed chart.

An illustration of the progressed potential is found in the chart of Princess Diana at her recent untimely death. Born at 7:45 PM on July 1, 1961 in Sandringham, England, her natal 8th house held a trio of potential malefic planets along with the node, which emphasised the configuration that fairly outlined the possibility of an untimely death. Of these 8th house planets, Mars and Pluto were in conjunction, and Mars ruled her 4th house of endings. Uranus suggested the sudden fashion in which she would depart.

Princess Diana's progressed chart showed that the progressed Ascendant was forming an exact conjunction with natal Saturn, and transiting Neptune was stimulating the pair by exact conjunction. The progressed Midheaven was forming an exact square to the 8th house North Node and not far from exact to progressed Uranus, also in the 8th. A natal square between Jupiter and Neptune was stimulated by both transiting Mars and Uranus, with Mars on Neptune, an aspect of the bizarre and often reflecting upon extreme physical discomfort.

Transiting Uranus along with Jupiter were opposing her progressed Sun in the 8th house. The transiting North Node was conjunct her progressed Mars, an aspect that frequently coincides with great activity, often involving force or conflict.

Princess Diana's chart also showed progressed Venus in conjunction with natal retrograde Mercury. Without going through the remaining contacts, the one that is most outstanding came from transiting Pluto, which formed an exact square to her natal Mars/Pluto conjunction in the 8th house, which at the same time had transiting Sun and Mercury in conjunction. The exact square from Pluto to Mars stimulated their natal relationship and the transits of both the Sun and Mars acted as the final trigger to set off events that tragic night. Aside from the alarming activity into the 8th house, Neptune was prominent, ruling photographers, alcohol, darkness and night time, and it is often involved when travel is an issue. Research has shown that when events take place of an untimely fashion, such as the illustration just given, or in cases of rape, kidnapping, and other events in which the individual appears to have little control, very powerful transits often appear to dominate the chart. Frequently it is found that there is a great amount of nodal activity, and Mars or Pluto is generally involved.

Once the progressed chart and the transiting planets have been considered for the current potential and major themes, the Solar and Lunar Returns can be read from a more authoritative level. They help determine when and how events will unfold. Predominant themes showing in the progressed chart will also show in the returns, usually becoming angular at such times that events associated with the theme are about to take place. Configurations will form that match progressed aspects and this may be either aspects formed among the return planets themselves, or between a return and natal planet.

Once the progressed chart and the transiting planets have been considered for the current potential and major themes, the Solar and Lunar Returns can be read from a more authoritative level. They help determine when and how events will unfold. Predominant themes showing in the progressed chart will also show in the returns, usually becoming angular at such times that events associated with the theme are about to take place. Configurations will form that match progressed aspects and this may be either aspects formed among the return planets themselves, or between a return and natal planet.

10.1. SOLAR AND LUNAR RETURNS

One of the most valuable contributions from the Solar and Lunar Returns is the way in which they enable one to narrow down the timing of events. This is in addition to indicating current environmental factors and the trend that personal experiences will take over the next year. A chart calculated for the exact time of the Sun's return to its natal position will result in an accurate map of the year to come. A Lunar Return is calculated the same way, except it is the return of the Moon to the exact degree and minute that it held in the natal horoscope and this chart is predictive of the four weeks to follow.

Interpreting the return charts is very similar to reading a natal chart, with the exception that all of the patterns showing in a return chart will develop to full maturity in a very short period of time, rather than over the course of a lifetime. The Solar Return works as a sort of auxiliary natal chart, each for just one year. The chart patterns show the foundation from which one will be working to follow the basic life purpose. This point in time is an important part of the life cycle and the resulting chart shows how the stage is set.

If the progressed configurations have been considered, it becomes a much simpler task to predict specific events. By knowing the underlying plot to the story, as shown in the progressions, it is easier to extract the major themes as they recur in the return chart, and judgement of particular aspects is more accurate. For example, one might be dismayed to find Saturn on an angle of the Solar Return, especially if in hard aspect to another planet. But unless the progressed chart shows the formation of several exact stressful aspects with Saturnine undertones, such a configuration is no reason for worry. It likely signals delays or a challenge to be overcome.

Because the Sun is the most important feature in a nativity, describing the character, ego drive, and destiny of the individual, the Solar Return can be used to find events in the near future that are of great significance on the pathway of life. Any planets falling on an angle of the Solar Return are of highest priority and show events coming within the year that reflect the nature of such a planet. If there are found to be exact angular placements of the natal planets, by inserting these onto the Solar Return wheel, they too are of high priority. The new chart is showing that conditions are ideal for the energies of that natal planet to manifest. The angles always provide an outlet for planetary energies.

One of the best auspices to look for in the Solar Return is a well aspected Sun. This provides for greater ease in pursuing one's life direction in the year that follows. The vitality is unencumbered, and assistance will come through others along the way. Adverse aspects to the Sun provide testimony to the types of challenges that will be encountered, as described by the planet in aspect. Having Jupiter, Venus, or the Sun on an angle of the chart and well aspected is a year to look forward to! Unless there are major countering themes, the year will bring great happiness and benefits.

Since the Moon is an important indicator of the daily tempo of life and reflects upon personal fluctuations, using the Solar and Lunar returns together is far more revealing than using either of them alone. Just as the natal horoscope is used as a foundation in reading progressions and transits, the Solar Return chart can be used to interpret the 13 Lunar Returns which fall within the year over which it presides.

When a Lunar Return closely matches the Solar Return by house cusps and house placements of the outer planets, a climatic four weeks will follow. In fact, this is likely to be the month in which the most important yearly events will take place. The most eventful period of the year will often find the same degree rising in the Lunar Return that was rising in the Solar Return. The Lunar Return Sun falling on an angle of the Solar Return also indicates an eventful period. When the Lunar Return Sun falls on a degree that activates an important Solar Return configuration, major yearly events indicated by the specific grouping will occur.

Rather than simply referring to the motion of the Sun through the Solar Return, top consideration should be given the degree it holds in the Lunar Return. This is another cyclic point, and the exact placements of planets in the return charts are far more potent than simple transits. This technique of superimposing the Lunar Return chart upon the Solar Return will supplement the Lunar Return chart reading. Detailed information comes to light through exact links made between the two charts that would otherwise go unnoticed, and timing can be better established.

For example; if a marriage ceremony is indicated in the Solar Return, it will be most likely to take place when the Lunar Return Sun lines up with the Solar Return 7th house. Of course, other planetary activity must be considered. Venus and Mars together in the sign of Libra or positioned together in the 7th or 10th house of the Lunar Return would also be appropriate indicators for such an event. The marriage may be the individual's own or someone else's, and such details can be found among the remaining chart indicators.

Similarly, being put in the spotlight career-wise is most likely to occur during the time period in which the Sun travels through the 10th house of the Solar Return. Events along these lines will be quite spectacular if the Lunar Return for the period finds the Sun on the cusp of the Solar Return 10th house. The days to expect the most activity during the Lunar Return period are when the Moon transits the angles of this chart.

A New or Full Moon appearing in either return chart has special significance. The New Moon shows the birth of something new and a sort of congealing of separate energies into one area that stimulates enthusiasm. The sign and house position of the New Moon gives the details, and unless there are many adverse aspects to the configuration, it is usually one to look forward to. The Full Moon is indicative of the completion of something and again it usually shows the culmination of a cooperative effort in accordance with the signs and houses involved. A Full Moon is slightly more inclined to signify an unfavourable event than a New Moon.

The first natal planet to rise to the Ascendant of any return chart will usually set the precedence for events to follow, with the Sun, Venus, and Jupiter inclining to favours, benefits, and pleasant social affairs. Saturn indicates business dealings, issues involving authorities, and possible delays involving important matters. Each of the planets will stamp their personal signature to the time period when first to rise.

A heavily tenanted sign or house will often lead the chart according to sign characteristics and/or issues pertaining to the emphasised house. Elemental prominence as well as hemispheric prominence should also be considered. A sign's mode of expression will influence the particular house that it rules. The fixed signs show permanence and stabilising qualities, mutable signs show fluctuations, and cardinal signs show personal action. Blending the elements with these shows an accent on the initiation of activity if a fire sign; on intellectual affairs if an air sign; and on psychological issues if a water sign. Further consideration of the particular sign will bring even more definition to each of the houses.

The houses of the return in which important natal planets fall also reveal details about the ensuing time period. If a return planet falls on a natal planet, then significant events relating to the house occupied by the pair will find the two planetary natures working together, either in harmony or discord. This is determined by the natal relationship of these planets and by the aspects made to them in the return.

In addition to the major themes showing in a return, a multitude of details adds up to a big picture. For instance, the area of the natal chart that is found occupying the 12th house of the Lunar Return is an area that is temporarily closed off from the individual, sort of in exile. There is an element of mystery here; maybe a secret or a missing piece of important data.

If it is the natal 2nd house lying within the boundaries of the 12th house of the Lunar Return, the individual may need to refrain from disclosing a financial matter or may be waiting to learn the outcome of a financial issue. This blending technique can be used for each of the houses in the return chart with reference to the traditional house meanings.

If a planet in the return is within a degree of forming a sextile or trine to the 2nd house cusp, the planet represents a line of assistance to one's income and resources, both private and cooperatively, since the 8th house cusp would also be favourably aspected. This would be the same with any planet to any house cusp, and an exact adverse aspect would show a block or challenge to the affairs of the house it is linked to. The nature of the planet along with the people and things it rules will reveal the particular type of assistance or challenge.

Wherever Gemini is found in the Solar or Lunar Return indicates an area of duplicity or multiplicity. If found on the 2nd house cusp, there may be income from two or more sources; if on the 7th, two experts may need to be consulted; if on the 6th, one may hold two jobs or be spread very thin to meet service obligations. The mutable signs always show areas that are undergoing fluctuation; whereas fixed signs show stability, and cardinal signs show initiative and enterprise.

If one of the inner planets rules the Ascendant, and is retrograde at the onset of the return, the chance for significant personal reversals is increased. This guideline can be extended to reveal potential reversals in the area of the chart ruled by Mercury, Venus, or Mars, if retrograde at the onset of the return.

Interceptions are important, since they may limit an outflow of energy involving the natal houses intercepted. For example, having the 6th and 12th natal houses intercepted in the 1st and 7th of the Return could show health/hospitalisation issues. This particular enclosure of the 6th/12th axis shows that health/hospitalisation matters will find an outlet through the 1st and 7th houses. The 1st reflects a physical outlet and the 7th suggests that the "other people" for the time period may be the doctors and hospital personnel as signified by the 12th.

Of course, in this particular illustration, there would be several additional indicators of illness in both the Solar and Lunar returns, and this bit of evidence would be useful to corroborate other findings. Look to the house position of the rulers of intercepted signs for an outlet of energies.

If one of the Moon's nodes falls in conjunction with a return planet, that planet will manifest more dynamically than usual, and issues associated with it will be of increased importance during the return period. The North Node falling on the Ascendant of the return provides many benefits for the period. One is easily able to lead and set the pace; and personal timing is excellent for gaining the support and cooperation of others.

Upcoming eclipses should be noted in case they stimulate an important configuration or point in the return chart. They are quite powerful even if occurring on a house cusp. In addition to the enormous significance of the nodes and eclipses, there are a few other specialised points that reveal great detail when found emphasised in the returns. The Aries Point, which actually includes the first degree of any of the cardinal signs, as well as a fixed group of stars called the Pleiades, are two of these specialised points. The Pleiades are located near the last degree of Taurus.

11

MODERN ASTROLOGY

A new astrology has been discovered. At the same time that the Hubble telescope is bringing us mind-expanding glimpses of our universe, there has quietly emerged a new conceptual way of looking at that universe. Paralleling advances in the various sciences, a new astrology has begun to replace the old.

The old astrology—the currently popular geocentric art that reached its high point during the Middle Ages—adequately described an old way of life. The grounded, earth-centered point of view was good enough for our ancestors in their reality—but it is no longer very useful.

Knowing, as we do, that the earth is not the center of everything, changes everything. We are a people—on a planet, orbiting a star, inside a galaxy, amongst countless galaxies like grains of sand. After a long history of living provincially and barbarically on planet earth, we are about to launch forth into the universe, quickly becoming intelligent birds of space that go on and on into the Void. Humanity is so amazed at this truth that it has reacted in shock and denial, and is trying to fall back to the past—hurriedly and forgetfully denying the new opportunity and staunchly attempting to carry on as usual with outmoded ways. However, the time for change has come—and we, reluctant or not, are definitely on our way to Infinity.

11.1. GALACTIC ASTROLOGY

Galactic astrology has evolved from the old astrology as a guide for the new humanity. Galactic astrology reminds that a human being's life is intermixed with the life of his planet, the life of his star, and the life of his galaxy. Instead of waiting until scientists get around to proving that the universe is totally conscious and alive, we affirm it now, and say, "As above, so below; we are a part of this divine cosmos. Let us behave accordingly."

And while we prepare for the stars, yet we still live solidly on earth. Galactic astrology is practical, providing help where we need it—in our everyday lives, in growing as human beings, in understanding our very important relationships, in making a decent living. This science helps us to dream great dreams, but it also takes care of the very real down-to-earth necessities which we all require.

Galactic astrology has been researched experimentally. Its findings have been slowly extracted from actual studies of history, historical personages, and present lives. It is built upon theory that matches the latest scientific discoveries, and then it is backed up with repeatable scientific proof.

A higher point of view leads to a higher life. Looking at your galactic chart of conception, we can see the high life that you may live—if you choose to live nobly and become high. We also can see the lower life, the common collective life that you might join—if you follow the crowd and give up. Both ways of life, the higher and the lower, are clearly visible in the galactic chart. By studying and understanding this chart, you are studying and understanding a higher view of yourself, with the result that you learn how to skillfully avoid the traps while you gladly reach for what is useful and happy.

As always, it is up to you, your own self-aware self, as you find yourself poised in the middle of the Stars, looking around with awe and wonder. Perhaps it is time for you to acknowledge that this beautiful cosmic mystery is worthy of utter respect, and so to live in the midst of it as as the wide-eyed child of a mighty Universe. Since that Universe is your real progenitor, your true mother and father, perhaps it is also time to understand that there is no end to wisdom, or to your growth.

Around the year 1750, astrology all but died out in Western culture. With the advent of scientific developments, the geocentric system upon which astrology was based gave way to the heliocentric vision of Copernicus. At the same time, scientists expounded greater and greater skepticism of some of the tenets of astrology as it was being practiced at the time. There are two principal arguments against astrology.

First, astrology could not be proven through the use of scientific experimental methods. While there is ample anecdotal evidence to confirm that people benefit from astrology, there are few, if any, studies to show how astrology works. Even today, there are only isolated cases in which astrological factors appear to have statistical significance.

Second, the Catholic Church has long taught that if astrology is not the direct work of the devil, then it is certainly an infringement upon individual free will. After all, astrology's detractors say that if we are fated to act in a certain way, that means that God has not given us free will. Since the Scriptures teach us that we have free will, astrology must be wrong.

11.2. ELECTIONAL ASTROLOGY

Electional astrology can be used to shed light on any planned event. You can choose a time to begin any activity that has an obvious time of origination. It would be difficult for most of us to pin down the exact onset of psychological or emotional conditions, and much easier to say when we graduated from high school, broke a bone or got married. Because electional astrology is an aid to future planning, you can create charts for a variety of dates and times. You can examine each chart for its benefits and detriments in regard to your intended goal. If nothing else, in the process you may examine your own motives, confirm your own feelings and organize your decision-making process more consciously. You affirm your intention.

Electional astrology provides a way to gain perspective on the design of our universe in a useful way. When faced with formidable problems, we can use the information provided by electional astrology to help us make a decision, not to make the decision for us. If god and goddess are behind all creation, then certainly they are behind the movements of the stars and planets.

SUGGESTED READINGS

Culver, R. B., and Ianna, P. A., *Astrology: True or False?*, New ed.: Buffalo, New York, Prometheus Books, (1988).

Cyril Fagan, *Primer of Sidereal Astrology,* Littlejohn, 1971.

Gopesh Kumar Ohja, *Hindu Predictive Astrology,* Taraporevala, Bombay, 1972.

Horasastra by Varahamihira. Adyar Library 1950. Sanskrit text of Varahamihira's classic work.

Keith Hutchison, "Towards a political iconology of the Copernican revolution", in Patrick Curry (ed), *Astrology, Science and Society: historical essays,* Woodbridge, 1987, 95-141.

Peter Burke, The fabrication of Louis XIV, New Haven, 1992

Raman, *Manual of Hindu Astrology* by IBH Prakashana, 10th edition, 1976.

R. S. Westman, "The astronomer's role in the sixteenth century: a preliminary study", *History of Science* 18, 105-47, (1980).

Tamsyn Barton, *Ancient Astrology,* London and New York, 1994

Other Books on

OCCULT SCIENCE